Contents

PART ONE: THE MONETARY ENVIRONMENT

Chapter Four

Chapter Five

Chapter Six

Chapter Seven

PART TWO: TECHNICAL ASPECTS

PART THREE: CASE STUDIES

PART FOUR: MAKING THE CHANGE

Acknowledgements

The Editors thank all the authors for their diligence and enthusiasm for this project. We are also grateful to friends, colleagues and fellow conference-goers who have helped shape our ideas during many discussions; and to the European Commission and the Association for Monetary Union in Europe.

Our secretaries, Aude Glénisson and Rachel Parry, have been entirely helpful.

Our publishers, the Federal Trust, have at all times been encouraging and efficient.

Finally, Sally Bishop and Edmée van Tuyll are to be much thanked for putting up with hours of cross-border e-mails and faxes.

The Federal Trust acknowledges support for
User Guide to the Euro from:
Banque Indosuez
The European Commission
Salomon Brothers International

About the Authors

Françoise Billon is an economist at the Banque à la Caisse Nationale de Crédit Agricole (CNCA), with special responsibility for EMU.

Graham Bishop, an editor, is Adviser on European Financial Affairs at Salomon Brothers International Ltd in London. He has also been a member of the European Commission's Consultative Group on the Impact of the Introduction of the Euro on Capital Markets, Chairman of the enquiry of the London Investment Banking Association (LIBA) on converting London's capital markets to the single currency, and a member of the Commission's Committee of Independent Experts on the preparation of the changeover to the single currency (the Maas Committee).

Henk Brouwer has been Treasurer-General of the Dutch Ministry of Finance since 1992 and is responsible for general economic and financial policy as well as monetary affairs. In July 1997 he will become a Director of the Dutch Central Bank.

John Chown is Chairman of J.F. Chown & Co. Ltd. He specialises in the international tax aspects of multi-currency financing and derivatives, and has written and lectured extensively on international tax and economics.

David Croughan is Chief Economist with the Irish Business and Employers Confederation and is responsible for economic and taxation policy. He is in charge of IBEC's information campaign on the changeover to the single currency.

Walter Dilewyns joined Agfa-Gevaert N.V. at the beginning of 1988 and is responsible for the treasury at the company's headquarters and at Agfa-Gevaert International N.V.

Pierre Duquesne was Deputy Director, in charge of multilateral affairs in the French Treasury (Ministry of Economics and Finance) until September 1996, where he was also chairman of the working group of the Monetary Committee on the adaptation of public administrations to the use of the single currency. He is now Deputy General Secretary of the Banking Commission.

Santiago Fernández de Lis is Deputy Head of International Economic Research at the Banco de España, in charge of analysis of international economic developments, in particular ERM and EMU issues.

Louis Frère is Financial and IT Director of GIB Group. He started his career in an audit firm, then worked for Chemical Bank and Solvay Group before joining GIB in 1987.

Alberto Giovannini is Senior Adviser at Long Term Capital Management, Research Associate of the National Bureau of Economic Research and Research Fellow of the Centre for Economic Policy Research (London). His most recent book, *The Debate on Money in Europe*, was published by MIT in 1996.

Sophie Goblet is Treasurer of GIB Group. Before that she worked for ABN-Amro Bank in Amsterdam and London.

Steve Green is Marketing Manager for Mars Electronic International, based in the UK, with responsibility for the European vending market. He is a Chartered Manufacturing Engineer.

xii   User Guide to the Euro

Graham Harvey is a Divisional Director of Marks & Spencer with responsibility for relations with EU institutions. He is leader of the UK delegation to CCD, the official liaison committee between commerce and the Commission.

Andreas Henkel joined the Federal Economic Chamber of Austria in 1985, where he is responsible for tax and financial policy. He is a member of the Economic and Fiscal Committee of UEAPME and coordinator of its working group on EMU.

Claus Hilles is the departmental head responsible for international business at Dresdner Bank AG in Frankfurt. He coordinates the bank's preparations for EMU.

Rolf Kaiser is an economic adviser in the European Commission and is responsible for Public Administration aspects of EMU.

Silvana Koch-Mehrin, a freelance journalist, is undertaking doctoral research on the Latin Monetary Union and currently holds a scholarship of the Friedrich-Naumann Foundation.

Jouko Kuisma works for the Kesko group, Finland's largest wholesale and retail group, and represents the Finnish Federation of Commerce and Trade in the EMU working group set up by the Ministry of Finance.

André Leysen became President of the Agfa-Gevaert Group in 1979 and since July 1987 has been Chairman of its Supervisory Board. He is also Vice-Chairman of the European Round Table of Industrialists.

Ian Lynch is a senior consultant with IBM Consulting Group. He had previously worked for the Barclays Group on financial EDI and international cash management.

Reine-Claude Mader is Secretary General of the Confédération Syndicale du Cadre de Vie (CSCV) as well as member of the Conseil National de la Consommation and Conseil National du Crédit.

Alec Nacamuli is Principal for payments services at IBM Consulting Group. Previously he worked at SWIFT, the worldwide network that supports international banking transactions.

José Pérez, an editor, is General Manager of Banco Bilbao Vizcaya and Head of Global Markets. He was previously General Manager of the Banco de España, responsible for Banking Supervision. He is a former Associate Professor at Universidad Complutense in Madrid.

Christian Pfister is Deputy Head of the Monetary Research and

Statistics Division of the Banque de France. He is a member of the Monetary Policy Sub-Committee of the EMI.

José Antònio Pires is marketing director of the Fábrica Leiriense der Plásticos S.A. and Board Director of Group Plasteuropa Holding.

Salvatore Rebecchini is Deputy Director of the Research Department of the Banca d'Italia. He is also a member of the Foreign Exchange Policy Sub-Committee of the EMI.

Leo van der Tas is a Senior Manager with Moret Ernst & Young Accountants and also Professor of Financial Reporting at Erasmus University in Rotterdam.

Jacques Terray is a partner at Gide Loyrette Nouel in charge of banking where he specialises in securities.

Sammy van Tuyll van Serooskerken, an editor, is Economic Adviser to the Director General for Economic and Financial Affairs at the European Commission, charged with EMU matters. He worked previously with the Ministry of Finance in the Netherlands, where he was head of the National Monetary Affairs Division, and at the Dutch Central Bank. He has written widely on monetary affairs, and teaches at the Université Libre de Bruxelles and is Secretary of the Tindemans Group on European Institutions.

Pascale Valent is in charge of managing preparations for the euro at the Crédit Agricole in the area of information systems.

Pierre Valentin has worked for Compagnie Parisienne de Réescompte since 1989 and is currently Head of International fixed income proprietary trading.

Leo Verwoerd is the director of the debt issuing Agency of the Ministry of Finance of the Netherlands. He has served as a member of the National Forum for the Introduction of the Euro and is former President of the Financial Action Task Force on Money Laundering.

José Viñals is currently Head of Economic Studies of the Banco de España and a Research Fellow of the Centre for Economic Policy Research (CEPR). He served previously with the Committee of Governors of the Central Banks of the European Community.

Dick Westendorp has been Director of the Consumentenbond since 1982. He is also Secretary of the Council of Consumers International.

Peter Wolf-Köppen works for Commerzbank AG in Frankfurt am Main. He is currently chairman of an intra-group steering committee for the change to the euro.

GLOSSARY

ATM	Automatic Teller Machine
ATS	Austrian Schilling
BEF	Belgian Franc
CAP	Common Agricultural Policy
CGT	Capital Gains Tax
DG	Directorate-General
DKR	Danish Kroner
DM	Deutschmark
EBRD	European Bank for Reconstruction and Development
EC	European Community
ECB	European Central Bank
ECBS	European Committee for Banking Standards
Ecu	European Currency Unit
EDP	Electronic Data Processing
EEA	European Economic Area
EEC	European Economic Community
EFTA	European Free Trade Area
EFTPoS	Electronic Fund Transfer at Point of Sale
EIB	European Investment Bank
EMI	European Monetary Institute
EMS	European Monetary System
EMU	Economic and Monetary Union
ERM	Exchange Rate Mechanism
ESCB	European System of Central Banks
EU	European Union
EUR	European Union Euro
EuroIBOR	Euro Inter Bank Offered Rate
EVA	European Vending Association
FATF	Financial Action Task Force
FFr	French Francs
FIM	Finnish Mark
GDP	Gross Domestic Product
GRD	Greek Drachma
IBAN	International Bank Account Number
IBEC	Irish Business and Employers Confederation
IEP	Irish Punt
IGC	Intergovernmental Conference

IPMA	International Primary Market Association
ISDA	International Swap and Derivatives Association
IT	Information Technology
ITL	Italian Lira
Kwh	Kilowatt hours
MDB	Multi-Drop Bus
NC	National Currency
NLG	Netherlands Guilders
OECD	Organisation for Economic Cooperation and Development
PIBOR	Paris Inter Bank Offered Rate
PTE	Portugese Escudo
SEK	Swedish Kroner
SME	Small and Medium-Sized Enterprise
SWIFT	Society for Worldwide Interbank Financial Telecommunication
TARGET	Trans-European Automated Real-Time Gross-Settlement Express Transfer
VAT	Value Added Tax
VMC	Vending Machine Controller

Foreword by
Mr Yves-Thibault de Silguy

*European Commissioner for Economic
and Financial Affairs*

The countdown has begun. The clock is ticking. On 1 January 1999, the euro will become Europe's single currency. This is a crucial step in the process of European integration, which will be important for all companies, big and small. Businesses have already seen the advantages of European integration in the form of the single market. It seems like long ago that most markets in Europe were separated by rigid differences before the innovations of the single market. The next generation of business and financial planners will find it hard to envisage the time when they operated in different currencies, just as we could not imagine what the US would look like with fifteen different sets of notes and coins.

Companies will soon start to benefit from the advantages of a more integrated and transparent economic environment. The euro will open up new markets, with a fresh boost to competition. Customers will be able to compare prices more easily and companies will be able to plan investment in a truly European currency. For intra-community trade, which represents for example 68% of total manufacturing trade in member states, the disappearance of exchange rate differences will simplify transactions and reduce surcharges. Finally, the euro will become a major currency for global transactions, helping to reinforce the competitiveness of European firms which for the first time will enjoy the advantages that their US counterparts have today of carrying out their business in a major global currency.

Preparing for the introduction of the euro is a huge challenge, requiring the partnership of the private and public actors at all levels: local, national and European. By reducing any remaining uncertainties about progress towards the euro, public authorities and market participants can help ensure a smooth transition. Member states have shown their commitment to the success of the euro by focusing their efforts on achieving economic convergence, and meeting the conditions set out in the Treaty. The Commission has also been working on how monetary union will operate once the euro is up and running and how companies, markets and public administrations should prepare themselves. Essential elements of the work include the new exchange rate mechanism and the stability pact, which will make security, credibility and solidarity a permanent feature of the euro zone, giving businesses the strong economic background they need to succeed. Current work also includes regulations defining the legal status of the euro so that companies can plan their own individual changeover with legal certainty.

Companies will have to undergo many changes, drawing up strategies to make the most of the opportunities that the euro will bring. Each firm and sector faces different challenges. The costs of transition are an investment in the future and it is worth preparing early, by keeping abreast of the latest developments on the road to the introduction of the euro and by addressing the nuts and bolts of the technical issues. The businesses which are the first to prepare themselves will reap the greatest competitive rewards. I welcome the initiative of this book in that it addresses specific technical details, and also serves as a rich quarry of ideas and a stimulus to remaining areas of debate. As such, it encapsulates the partnership of the public and private sectors across Europe needed for a smooth and successful transition to the euro.

Foreword by Mr Etienne Davignon

President of the Association for the
Monetary Union of Europe and
President of Société Générale de Belgique

I believe the decision to achieve EMU in 1999 is a decisive step in European history which has not just been achieved for the sake of creating monetary stability. In facing today's global marketplaces, EMU is meant to restore economic growth and contribute to maintain peace and public welfare in the world. But the public confronted with unemployment remains highly sceptical.

The Treaty of Rome signed in 1957 had already set out the fundamental principles of an European economic union. These consist today of four components:

1. a single market;
2. common policies in the field of competition;
3. regional and structural common policies;
4. the coordination of national economic policies, including fiscal policies.

Under the blueprint of the Maastricht Treaty, European monetary union will be given credibility and permanence through the introduction of the euro, which is the only way to take full advantage of the single market. In the absence of a single currency, the European single market would remain weakened by currency volatility that could lead to protectionist policies. When introduced, the single currency, the revised European Monetary System, and the forthcoming stability pact will eradicate exchange rate uncertainties.

The key element which will give a strong impetus to the coordination of monetary and fiscal policies will be the stability pact. The European Council in Dublin which will be held in December 1996 is expected to adopt the stability pact principles. Once EMU has started it will guarantee, among major effects, a durable monetary stability. It is therefore important to agree on mechanisms aimed to reinforce budgetary discipline.

EMU is becoming more and more a reality. Many practical issues have already been solved. From Maastricht to Madrid, EMU has been a process on the constant move which has handled the various aspects for a successful transition, notwithstanding several monetary crises in Europe.

The success of monetary union depends on adequate practical and technical preparations. The decisions taken by the European Council in Madrid on the scenario for the introduction of the single currency and its name, the euro, were of crucial importance. They sent a clear signal about the political commitment to the process, which proved vital for the confidence of the private sector actors, who then started actively preparing for the changeover.

Much is now expected from the Dublin summit in December 1996 which should ensure the durability of a stable monetary relationship between all members of the EU.

It is now important that each member state adopts communication strategies that will create understanding and confidence about EMU among the general public. This is perhaps the biggest challenge of all. Technical problems always find technical solutions, but the human dimension is non-tangible. EMU is the first project in the history of the European construction which will directly affect the lives of all individuals, and many of these still have to be convinced that present efforts to curb inflation and public deficits will effectively lead to increased public well-being.

The single currency will be at the centre of Europe's political agenda at the start of the next millennium. Economic and Monetary Union, institutional reform and further enlargement to meet the legitimate demand of East European countries, are the three main challenges of the years ahead. EMU therefore provides the most promising area for progress in the immediate future. It will demand determination and commitment to achieve this historic goal. Preparations will intensify and progressively extend to new areas as we approach the fixing of parities on 1 January 1999.

Economic and Monetary Union will fulfill an aspiration which was formed more than forty years ago. It will bring together the political vision or a more united Europe with the economic ideal of monetary stability. As the necessary achievement for this end of century EMU will result in a truly integrated European economy.

EMU is designed to re-establish economic growth and confidence in the European market. As a result, it will bring many advantages to the consumers. Better price transparency, lower interest rates, cheaper goods and services, a larger volume of exports will be the major effects of this new economic era.

Monetary union is the will of European countries and peoples to share their efforts and resources toward the same goal. This is a unique opportunity which we cannot miss to strengthen the economic and political stability as well as the public well-being in the world. This is a chance that all of us Europeans must take with all our hearts. Because it is only through EMU that Europe will reinforce its position in today's global economy, and will be accepted as a major player by the rest of the world.

Introduction to the User Guide

When this book is published, in the second half of December 1996, there will be hardly 500 business days before the start of monetary union on 1 January 1999. The introduction of the euro will affect the everyday life and work of millions of people and firms throughout the world. *User Guide to the Euro* tells the story of how this revolution is to take place and what should be done to prepare for it. It is a practical book written by experts with a deep knowledge of the imminent currency conversion.

We explain the background to the single currency. Anticipated problems are frankly discussed and solutions clearly presented. Examples of best practice are shared in both wholesale and retail sectors. The special needs of multi-nationals, small firms, banks and shops are addressed. This book is an essential companion for those preparing their enterprises for the changeover to the euro.

We have tried to be as practical as possible, but there are no tailor-made solutions for every problem and situation. The issues are complicated, and every firm is different. Even though many issues have been settled and companies are already making plans for the changeover to the euro on the basis of what has been decided so far, many other issues are still unresolved. The transition to the single currency is a continuing process: new solutions will have to be found for new problems as they arise.

The name *User Guide* suggests that it has been written for everyone who at some stage will start using the euro. In principle this means 370 million European citizens. But it is probably too early to write for such a large audience and the issues discussed are too specific. The book is designed for those who are in charge of a company. A general manager may well have to explain in the next annual report the company's plans for the changeover. This book should give enough insight to make this plan. However, the book has also been written for a wider audience: it should appeal to everyone who is interested in the single currency and in the monetary future of their country.

We requested contributions from experts in different subjects to achieve both a high quality and also to illustrate different approaches. On certain issues, the experts even express divergent opinions.

The book is in four parts. Part One describes the monetary environment. It discusses why the EU wants to achieve monetary union; the three phases of the introduction of the euro; the stability of exchange rates; monetary policy in EMU; the impact on financial markets and the new exchange rate relationship between the 'ins' and the 'near-ins'.

Part Two discusses legal and technical aspects of the introduction of the single currency: and in particular the continuity of contracts; the payment systems in the transitional period; accounting problems; taxation; software; dual pricing; converting vending machines and the logistics of changing the cash for the banking sector.

Part Three consists of different case studies. How do banks, multinational companies, small and medium enterprises, in particular in the retail sector, and a public administration prepare for the changeover? And how should consumers react? Part Four discusses the organisation of the changeover. Who will be responsible for what; how member states should organise the changeover and the role of trade associations.

At the end of the book we give some concluding remarks highlighting problems that have been identified by the individual authors. Some of these will require policy choice by governments. We also discuss some of the issues which shareholders may well wish to see reviewed in Annual Reports.

Each author wrote their chapter in a personal capacity. The views expressed are only those of the author and are not necessarily those of the company or institution from which they come. Moreover, the editors are not responsible for the views expressed by the authors.

The framework for EMU is now in place. This is the right time to publish this user guide. However, in a fast-developing story, some passages may already appear a little outdated. Wherever the solution chosen by the authors is not definitive, we say so. A further edition is planned to up-date the text.

We would welcome the views of our readers about this book. Constructive comments will help to make a second edition even more useful. They should be addressed to us at the Federal Trust, 11 Tufton Street, London SW1P 3QB.

The Editors
Brussels - London - Madrid
29 November 1996

PART ONE: THE MONETARY ENVIRONMENT

Chapter One

Background to Economic and Monetary Union

Graham Bishop, José Pérez and Sammy van Tuyll

For a quarter of a century before the signing of the Treaty of Maastricht in 1992, Economic and Monetary Union (EMU) has been a recurrent aim of the European Community. When the Community was set up, the international monetary system was that of Bretton Woods, which provided currency stability with the US dollar as the dominant monetary standard. This system began to show signs of weakness in the late 1950s. By 1968-69, revaluation of the Deutschmark and devaluation of the French franc threatened the stability of other European currencies. EMU therefore became a formal goal of the Community at the Hague summit in December 1969. A high level group, chaired by the Luxembourg prime minister, Pierre Werner, was asked to report on how EMU could be achieved by 1980.

The Werner report of October 1970 proposed a three stage process for achieving a complete EMU within a ten year period. The final objective would be the free movement of capital, the permanent locking of exchange rates or even the replacement of the currencies of the six member states by a single currency. In addition, Werner recommended a strengthening of economic policy coordination and even the setting of frameworks for national budgetary policies.

In March 1971, the Six agreed in principle on a three stage approach to EMU, even though they were divided over some of the report's main recommendations. The first stage, narrowing of exchange-rate fluctuations, was to be tried on an experimental basis, without commitment to the other stages.

The break-up of the Bretton Woods system and the floating of the US dollar in August 1971, affected exchange rate stability in

Europe. As a response, the Six created the 'snake in the tunnel', a mechanism for managing the fluctuations of European currencies (the snake) inside narrow limits against the dollar (the tunnel). The oil crisis, dollar weakness and policy divergence hampered exchange rate stability and within two years the snake was reduced to the German, Benelux and Danish currencies.

Interest in EMU had not disappeared. EMU was one of the proposals that Leo Tindemans, prime minister of Belgium, made in his 1975 report on European Union, though he acknowledged that it could only be a long run goal. In 1979, the European Monetary System (EMS) was launched, which was built on the concept of stable, but adjustable exchange rates. All the member states' currencies, with the exception of the British pound, joined its Exchange Rate Mechanism (ERM). It provided for a grid of bilateral rates and fluctuations that were not to exceed a margin of 2.25%. The EMS introduced a new currency, the ecu ('European currency unit') as a weighted average of all EMS currencies. The EMS succeeded in reducing exchange rate volatility, which between 1986-89, was a quarter of what it had been in 1975-79.

The 1985 programme for the completion of the single market aimed at removing all non-tariff barriers to the free movement of goods, persons, services and capital. It became clear, however, that the benefits of the internal market would be difficult to achieve with the uncertainties created by exchange rate fluctuations and the high transaction costs for converting one currency into the other. The single currency was seen as the vital missing piece in the single market project. Moreover, many economists pointed to the so-called impossible triangle: one may not have at the same time free capital movements, stable exchange rates and an independent monetary policy.

The European Council meeting at Hanover in June 1988 established a committee, chaired by the then President of the Commission, Jacques Delors, to study EMU. The Delors Committee included all EC Central Bank Governors and independent experts. Its report, submitted in April 1988, proposed to achieve EMU in three stages. The Madrid European Council of June 1989 decided to proceed to the first stage of EMU, the liberalisation of capital movements, in July 1990. In December 1989, the European Council decided in Strasbourg to convene an Intergovernmental Conference at the end of 1990 in order to negotiate a Treaty on Economic and Monetary Union. This Intergovernmental Conference, held in 1991, resulted in the Treaty on European Union, concluded in Maastricht in December 1991 and signed on 7 February 1992.[1]

The Maastricht Treaty

The Maastricht Treaty provides for monetary union to be achieved by the end of the century. A European System of Central Banks (ESCB) will be established, which will be in charge of conducting a single monetary policy. Its primary objective will be to maintain price stability. The ESCB will consist of the European Central Bank (ECB) and the national central banks of the member states. They will all be independent from Community (or now 'Union') institutions and the governments of the member states, so as to make sure that no other policy considerations interfere with the price stability objective.

Monetary union will be achieved in three stages. The first started on 1 July 1990, the second on 1 January 1994 and the final stage will start on 1 January 1999. On that day, the Council shall take all measures necessary for the rapid introduction of the single currency. The Treaty did not specify how and when the single currency should be introduced.

Economic policies of the member states will be regarded as a matter of common concern. They shall be based on the principle of an open market economy with free competition, favouring an efficient allocation of resources. One of the guiding principles of economic policy will be sound public finance. The Treaty introduced an 'excessive deficit procedure' to ensure that member states achieve, and maintain that soundness.

In early 1992, just after the signing of the Maastricht Treaty, it was generally expected that stability in the ERM would continue until monetary union had been achieved. In September 1992, however, speculation triggered by an initial 'no' in the Danish referendum of June on the Treaty and an uncertain outcome of a similar referendum in France, forced the Italian lira and then the British pound out of the ERM. Another currency crisis in July/August 1993 put the French franc under pressure and on 2 August 1993 it was decided to widen the fluctuation bands of the ERM to 15%. Some started doubting the feasibility of EMU.

Confidence in EMU returned when all member states had ratified the Treaty and it came into force on 1 November 1993. On 1 January 1994, Stage Two of EMU began formally and the European Monetary Institute (EMI) was established, a body charged with strengthening cooperation between the national central banks in preparation for the third stage of EMU.

The Commission set up an expert group on the changeover to the single currency in May 1994, with the remit of advising it on the technical preparations for introducing the single currency. This expert group was chaired by Cees Maas, a former chairman of the EU's Monetary Committee. On 31 May 1995, the Commission adopted the 'Green Paper on the practical arrangements for the introduction of the single currency'. This proposed to introduce the single currency in three phases and, together with an EMI report of 14 November on the 'Changeover to the single currency', formed the basis for the reference scenario decided at the Madrid meeting of the European Council on 15 and 16 December 1995.

The Madrid European Council
The Madrid Council took two important decision with respect to the single currency. First it decided that the name of the single currency would be the euro. Secondly, it decided to introduce the single currency in three phases. The first, phase 'A', will begin as early as possible in 1998, when the decision is taken about which member states fulfil the necessary conditions for the adoption of the single currency. Phase B will start on 1 January 1999 and is the beginning of Stage Three of EMU. Phase C will start on 1 January 2002 at the latest and will last six months at most. During this phase, euro notes and coins will be introduced. Chapter Three gives a detailed description of the introduction scenario and the timetable is set out in Appendix One.

In addition, the Madrid Council requested work to be done in three areas: (i) the legal framework for the introduction of the euro: the technical preparatory work of this should be completed by the end of 1996; (ii) a new exchange rate relationship between currencies of member states which are not immediately participating in monetary union (between the 'ins' and the nearly-in or 'pre-ins'); and (iii) a Stability Pact that will ensure that member states keep their commitment to sound public finances once they have entered monetary union.

As a consequence of the Madrid decisions, confidence increased tremendously that monetary union would be realised as planned. A very good indicator of financial market expectations about EMU is the long term interest rate differential between the Deutschmark and the French franc. In December 1995, this spread was about 60 basis points (0.6%). In the weeks after Madrid it disappeared completely and the rates of the FFr and the DM are now the same.

Moreover, preparations for the single currency have speeded up not only within the public sector, at both EU and member state level, but also in the private sector. In particular, many banks and larger enterprises have set up task forces to prepare for the changeover to the euro.

The European Council, meeting in Dublin on 13-14 December 1996, will discuss the legal framework, the exchange rate relations between the ins and pre-ins and the Stability Pact. With respect to the latter, consensus has been reached that member states should aim for budgets that are close to balance or in surplus. In addition, multilateral surveillance will be increased so as to make sure that any slippage of fiscal targets is monitored in a timely way: member states are to submit stability programmes in which they explain their budgetary positions and medium term outlook. The exchange rate relationship between the ins and pre-ins is discussed in Chapter Seven and the legal framework in Chapter Eight.

---

[1] For a full description of the Treaty of Maastricht, see Andrew Duff, John Pinder and Roy Pryce (eds), *Maastricht and Beyond: Building the European Union*, London, Routledge, 1994.

THE CHRONOLOGY OF EMU

1957, 25 March	Signing of the Treaty of Rome
1958, 1 January	Establishment of the European Economic Community
1969, December	The Hague Summit requests a report
1970, October	Werner Report
1972, March	Creation of the snake in the tunnel
1979, 13 March	Start of the European Monetary System
1988, June	European Council, Hanover requests a study
1989, April	Delors Committee Report
1992, 7 February	Signing of the Maastricht Treaty
1992, 2 June	Referendum in Denmark
1992, 20 September	Referendum in France
1993, 2 August	Widening of ERM fluctuation bands to 15%
1993, 1 November	Coming into force of the Maastricht Treaty
1994, 1 January	Beginning of Stage Two of EMU: establishment of EMI, prohibition of central bank credit to governments
1995, 31 May	European Commission Green Paper on the practical arrangements
1995, 14 November	EMI report on the changeover
1995, 15-16 December	European Council in Madrid
1996, 13-14 December	European Council in Dublin

Chapter Two

Why Monetary Union?

Alberto Giovannini

Very few people claim to know about the effects of monetary policy in the economy and those of alternative monetary systems. Indeed, even monetary theorists declare themselves at a loss in the effort to build a satisfactory and usable theory of money and monetary policy based on explicit assumptions on the organisation of markets. Yet, in the popular imagination, issues related to monetary policy stir very strong feelings. Economic and Monetary Union (EMU), undoubtedly the most important event in the economic history of Europe in the postwar period and a project that does not have precedents, has triggered dramatic debates between supporters and attackers, affected elections, spurred the creation of political parties and never ceased to excite commentators. And the clamour has increased as the date of EMU has drawn closer.

This chapter summarises the arguments most frequently heard in favour of EMU, and they are grouped into three classes: political arguments, arguments on the role of central banks and monetary policy and arguments on the economic role of money in the economy.

Political arguments

In the twentieth century, Europe has experienced devastating conflicts which threatened the very survival of western civilisation. Whole generations have been maimed by the two world wars and only now is the generation that was born after 1945 gaining charge of economic and political events.

One of the most important motors of the process of European integration, of which monetary union is the culmination, is the pursuit of peaceful and prosperous coexistence of European countries. The two pillars of that coexistence are believed to be solid free market institutions and the limitation of the powers of intervention of nation states.

The idea that free market institutions foster peace through economic prosperity was first exploited, in this century, in the negotiations between the US and Britain at the beginning of the second world war, and inspired the creation of the postwar economic institutions at Bretton Woods. This idea was further bolstered by the collapse of the non-market-based economic systems of Eastern Europe and the Soviet Union.

The idea that the role of the nation state in the economy has to be re-considered, and surely dramatically reduced, originates from the failures of economic policies, loosely inspired by Keynesianism. These were based on significant intervention by the government in economic activity and postulated 'mixed' economies where public and private ownership of economic activities could coexist. Such policies, pursued by the majority of industrial countries in the postwar period, have become financially unsustainable as economic growth has slowed down after the period of postwar reconstruction. In most cases, these policies have proven to be downright inefficient.

In the monetary and financial area, the heavy inheritance of interventionist nation states is especially visible. The European financial system is one where tax and regulatory havens coexist with relatively underdeveloped national financial markets. In the past, tax havens grew up as a result of overly restrictive financial regulations in individual countries, which, in turn, were the cause of the underdevelopment of many national financial markets.

In sum, the political underpinning of EMU is the idea that institutions that foster cooperation and prevent beggar-thy-neighbour policies, while at that same time supporting free international transactions of private market participants, are the key to maintaining a prosperous and peaceful Europe. The European Central Bank and the single European currency are viewed as devices to prevent the pursuit of policies which are in the short-run interest of individual countries or groups, but would, in total, cost Europe as a whole, by increasing friction among countries.

The role of central banks and monetary policy in Europe
The project of monetary union in Europe is also a conscious attempt to build a more efficient monetary system, by limiting the pressures in individual countries to effect economic activity through the use of monetary policy.

One of the few results in monetary theory on which there is little disagreement is that the repeated and systematic use of expansionist monetary policy leads only to inflation and, over time, has either negligible or negative effects on economic growth. In the case of European countries, more expansionist economic policies lead to exchange rate depreciations as well. Such depreciations, anticipated in the marketplace, are the cause of large and persistent interest rate differentials between European countries.

The big European problems of the moment are unemployment, an oversized and inadequate welfare system (and in particular an oversized yet inadequate social security system), and the persistence of large areas of market inefficiency, characterised by limited or non-existent competition.

In theory, all of these problems could be attacked with expansionist monetary policies. For example, a surprise monetary expansion would give rise to an exchange rate depreciation that would decrease relative wages in countries where monopolistic labour markets do not allow wages to reflect labour productivity and therefore induce high unemployment. The decrease in the international price of domestic output would give back the competitiveness lost by inefficient labour markets.

But none of these problems can be solved by expansionist monetary policies. In the exchange rate depreciation example above, anticipation of such policies would lead trade unions to set contractual wages in a way that would reflect the risk of depreciations. This would lead to persistent wage biases, would force periodic depreciations, and would induce high inflation in the long run, without really affecting the key problem, that is, the problem of non-competitive labour markets.

The 'right' policy responses are those that tackle such problems directly, for example reform of goods and labour markets as well as overhauling the welfare system.

The construction of a single, independent European Central Bank is a conscious attempt to defend monetary policy in Europe from the pressures to do things that monetary policy should not, and cannot, do. Whenever monetary policy is used to solve economic problems that are extraneous to its mandate (stable purchasing power, stable financial markets), it ends up creating additional distortions and imbalances (like the interest-rate differentials or the inflation bias in the example above).

The economic functions of money

The three functions of money are:

- *Standard of value measurement.* The use of a single yardstick for measurement of value simplifies the work of markets.

- *Means of payment.* A common exchange medium also adds value in the marketplace, by eliminating the problem of valuation of the goods or assets that could be received in exchange.

- *Store of value.* Although inferior to other forms of storing value (securities, for example), money carries value both across space and across time.

The creation of a single European money will enhance the first two functions: a single European currency will be the standard of measurement of a much wider set of goods and services. As such, it will facilitate more transparent markets and stronger competition.

In addition, a single European currency will be a very widely accepted means of payment. The result will be very large economies of scale in transactions, as well as the elimination of transaction costs that are now needed to convert one European currency into another.

Fears have been expressed that the new European currency will be less 'strong' than the strongest currency in Europe today and will thus display fewer qualities as a store of value. The Treaty of Maastricht has created a number of safeguards, including: measures to ensure sound fiscal policies, the independence of the European Central Bank; and the independence of national and European fiscal authorities from each other. These safeguards are designed to ensure that the third economic function of the European single currency, the store of value function, is as good as possible. Of course, inflation depends on inflationary expectations, and the latter reflects central bank credibility, which will only be established over time as the new central bank establishes a track record.

Thus, at least in the intentions of its creators, EMU will represent genuine technological progress in the economics of means of exchange. It will allow a fuller exploitation of efficiency gains arising from the widespread use of a single means of payment and unit of measurement, eventually in the whole of the European Union.

THE IMPACT OF THE CHANGEOVER TO THE EURO FROM A EUROPEAN MULTINATIONAL PERSPECTIVE

André Leysen

Multinational companies have a long experience of exchange rate fluctuations. Their operations will be made much easier by the introduction of the single currency.

The basic principles of the transition from national currencies to the euro were clarified at the Madrid European Council in mid-December 1995. From this the perspectives of the realisation of monetary union became more precise and concrete. The European Council in Florence in June 1996 concluded with a renewed pledge from the heads of government to launch EMU in 1999. These official statements confirm that the tide of political opinion (at least in continental Europe) is still flowing strongly in favour of EMU.

For multinational European companies, such as Agfa-Gevaert, this is basically good news. The switch to the single currency will offer some advantages and some disadvantages, but certainly opportunities. The impact will be difficult to quantify, but the changeover will undoubtedly affect the entire company. It will be felt from the macro environment to the micro level of the company; from top to bottom, and in virtually every functional group within the organisation.

In general, the euro should enable European companies to be more competitive in global markets. Why ?

Realisation of the European single market
The single currency is the next step towards the further integration and realisation of the European single market.

Having the backing of a sizeable and fully integrated home market is important to a multinational company, because international operations can then be built on a strong efficient organisation at home. This can be illustrated easily by the case of Agfa-Gevaert, whose two main competitors (Kodak and Fuji) benefit from achieving approx. 60% of their turnover in their integrated home markets. For Agfa-Gevaert this is less than 20% (Germany and Belgium).

Elimination of exchange rate instability

The considerable fluctuations, or more specifically, the competitive devaluation between some European currencies over the last two to three years have led to dramatic competitive distortions among manufacturers based in various member states of the Union. As these exchange rate fluctuations did not necessarily reflect economic fundamentals, but were more the consequence of what we can call 'psychological' shifts in the financial markets, they were difficult to deal with, especially when based in the 'heart' of Europe.

As a result, most affected industries called for protective or corrective measures and threatened to delocalise their activities and withhold investment decisions. This underlines why the euro seems to be the only way to make competition-distorting currency fluctuations a thing of the past. For a company it will:

- increase certainty and stability;
- eliminate the cost associated with exchange cover of the currencies involved which, in some cases, can account for a few percentage points of the cost of sales;
- eliminate a large number of transactions and associated costs.

Deeper and broader financial markets

In addition, volatility between the major anchor currencies of the dollar, Deutschmark and yen has escalated in recent years. One reason is that the DM has gained the status of an international anchor currency, which does not correspond with its economic weight. This has tended to make it the plaything of the financial markets. The broader euro currency area will enable Europe to play a monetary role that more closely reflects its economic and commercial status. The euro can fully exercise its role in a world monetary system characterised by progressive evolution towards a tripolar exchange rate mechanism. This effect, combined with elimination of exchange rate risk within the euro-zone, will decrease considerably the economic exchange rate risk of European multinational companies. The benefit for European companies will be that they become less vulnerable to instability in world financial markets.

Deeper and broader financial markets will also produce attractive investment and financing opportunities. Thanks to increased competition between financial institutions, European businesses will be able to choose from better offers and can appeal to financial instruments not available at the moment because of lack of liquidity. From an investor's point of view, opportunities will be available to build up a more diversified portfolio (without additional currency risk).

Price transparency
An additional effect of the single market and more specifically of the single currency will be more transparent prices. Without exchange rate movements and the confusion of different currencies at the distribution and retail level, competition will probably be more open and more focused on the fundamentals of cost, quality and service. Not every company, however, will enjoy this effect.

From a strictly marketing point of view price transparency will probably limit the companies' pricing policy and possibilities. On the other hand, the company will benefit from this effect in its purchasing operations. So the impact is very difficult to quantify and should not be overestimated as factors such as legal regulations, local taxation, cultural differences and business attitudes will certainly still contribute to market segmentation.

In the long run, price transparency will highlight differences between countries and could lead to a harmonisation of fiscal policies for example, and a convergence of business attitudes, such as terms of payment. Competition will be more intense and focused on fundamentals rather than on financial management.

When we speak about price transparency we also have to reflect on the fact that the single currency also brings wage transparency and more competition in the labour markets. Due to the elimination of the exchange rate factor, wage increases will have to reflect inflation and productivity growth more accurately.

Opportunity to redefine procedures and relations
To the benefits mentioned above we can add specific competitive advantages reserved for those companies which are creative enough to procure them. Indeed, the changeover to the single currency offers a unique opportunity to make the organisation more efficient. One of the most obvious functions which comes to mind is that of the treasury, which if not already centralised will be able to take advantage of the broader financial markets. But opportunities can also be found in logistics, marketing, administration and electronic data processing

(EDP) The introduction of the euro will also be an occasion to redefine relationships with all types of business partners, including clients, banks, suppliers and investors.

Risk factors and cost generators

Although the switch-over to the euro will offer a lot of advantages, we cannot blindly state that there are no risks or costs involved. The risk of non-introduction of the euro is often overstated: given the present economic and political climate, this should no longer be an obstacle to companies' preparations. However, the consequences of not introducing the euro cannot be overlooked: the effect in the financial markets would be very serious and would certainly lead to a loss of competitiveness for European companies. Other risks are more linked with the organisation of the company and relations with partners, such as if clients or suppliers do not accept the new currency, if there are ambiguities in contracts, if the EDP department is not ready with the necessary updates of the systems, or if the company has no real strategy in converting to the euro.

In order to reduce the risks involved companies should start in good time to prepare for the changeover. This will generate significant costs for updating data processing systems, for renewing and renegotiating contracts, and for internal and external communication, but these costs should be looked upon as a one-off cost, an investment for the future.

The burden of remaining uncertainties

There are still a lot of mostly technical uncertainties regarding the conditions and practicalities of the conversion process. Certainly the coexistence between two currencies in Phase B is a source of many questions and contingencies that complicates the switchover. We believe it essential that the political, administrative and economic protagonists in this conversion scenario work together to clarify the prevailing uncertainties as quickly as possible, and that a precise and stable legal and regulatory framework is provided.

It is also clear that the benefits highlighted above will not be realised if an insufficient number of currencies merge into the euro. In that case, the major problem of competitive devaluations of certain currencies is not solved. We are know that there are rules, treaties and economic realities which cannot be ignored, and it would be an illusion to believe that all European currencies can merge into the euro from day one. From this perspective the phases after the first introduction of the euro will be important. One may take heart from the fact that there is less talk now of the 'ins' and 'outs' but of 'ins' and 'pre-ins'. This indicates a strong desire to keep the convergence process going.

Monetary union and more specifically the introduction of a single currency will be a challenge to European companies. The opportunities offered can be summarised as the ability to rely on a more integrated single market and to reduce financial costs and exchange risk and the opportunity to simplify procedures and organisation. The inevitable costs, and risks, can only be minimised through thorough and early preparation and the working together of the different economic and regulatory agents.

OTHER MONETARY UNIONS

Silvana Kock-Mehrin

There were several interesting attempts in the nineteenth century to form monetary unions with a common coinage and currency system among a number of clearly distinct nation states. Since gold and silver were still the most important reference points in international commercial and financial relations, inflationary problems occurred almost only if there were new, major discoveries of these precious metals. Although the preference for using bank notes as a matter of convenience increased during that time, they remained related to gold or silver. Moreover, monetary policy and central banks were still in their infancy and hardly existed in the modern sense. Nevertheless, it is interesting to note that enthusiasm for monetary union is not new and history, though it does not repeat itself exactly, has produced variations on continuing themes.

The Austro-German monetary union 1857-1866
In 1857, Austria concluded a treaty with the members of the German Zollverein. There were three distinct currency units linked together at a stipulated constant rate of conversion and with a common unit of account. However, a common coin to replace all existing national currency units was not foreseen. There was no supranational agency, or agreed mode, for the settlement of disputes if the contracting

parties failed to meet their obligations. Without any real integration of the banking and monetary systems, the union remained only a formal obligation to maintain stipulated rates of exchange among the respective currencies. The union's dissolution was the result of a severe political conflict which erupted into war between Austria and Prussia in 1866.

The Latin monetary union 1865-1878

France initiated, and dominated, this important union with Belgium, Italy and Switzerland in 1865. The three latter countries had already adopted the French bimetallic standard with a fixed relation between silver and gold, so the basis for monetary cooperation existed already. The purpose of the treaty was to achieve uniformity of coinage. Thus the participants agreed to mint only coins of common weight, quality and diameter which would be reciprocally received by their public treasuries as legal tender. There was a provision which limited the issue to a formula based on respective population size.

The union could not continue to be successful because several factors were ignored: the increasing use of banknotes, which the treaty did not cover, and the temporary decline in the value of silver relative to gold. The unforeseen inflow of silver caught France and her partners in a silver vice. Whilst dealing with this problem, the weakness of an international monetary system without adequate mechanisms for coordination and problem-solving capacity became manifest. Hence in 1878, the entire union agreed to suspend silver coinage. This was the de facto end of the union, although it technically survived until after the first world war.

The Scandinavian monetary union 1875-1917

In 1875 Denmark, Norway and Sweden agreed to adopt identical styles of coins. The convention did not include any provisions for the inter-circulation of bank notes, although peoples of the Scandinavian countries during this era were already using bank notes for a great part of their transactions. Yet it soon became customary for the central banks of these countries to receive the notes of the others and forward them for credit to a current account maintained by each of the banks. The union thus succeeded in economising on gold transactions and establishing an efficient international clearing mechanism.

After 49 years of effective cooperation, the first world war had an unsettling effect on the economic and financial structure of the

Scandinavian countries. Disparities in their relative price structures and the massive inflow of gold led to disruptive effects in the respective exchange value of the three currencies. In 1917 the nations agreed to a mutual gold exclusion policy, thus marking the end of the Scandinavian monetary union.

The Belgian-Luxembourg Economic Union (BLEU)

The BLEU was established by a treaty in 1921. The Luxembourg franc was then tied to the Belgian franc at a one to one rate. During the second world war, occupied Luxembourg became a part of the German monetary area, but a treaty revision in 1944 reaffirmed the par value with the Belgian franc. A more detailed arrangement for monetary association further specified the framework of monetary cooperation within the BLEU in 1981. Hence Belgian banknotes and coins are legal tender in Luxembourg, whereas Luxembourg banknotes and coins are not legal tender in Belgium but can be exchanged without costs. The external value to all other currencies is identical. Exchange rate policy in relation to currencies of third countries is adopted by mutual agreement. Although economic data showed differences in the countries, this monetary union has continued to work successfully for more than 70 years.

Chapter Three

Introducing the Euro:
the Three Phases

Sammy van Tuyll

The Maastricht Treaty, which was signed in 1992, determined three stages for achieving monetary union. The first had already started in 1990 with the removal of any restriction on capital movement. Stage two began on 1 January 1994: the European Monetary Institute (EMI) was established and governments could no longer have overdraft facilities or any other type of credit facility with the central banks. The third stage of EMU will start on 1 January 1999. According to the Treaty, the exchange rates of the participating currencies will be irrevocably fixed, monetary policy will be conducted by the European Central Bank and the Council shall take the measures necessary for the rapid introduction of the single currency. The Treaty does not, however, determine how and when the single currency will be introduced. This was decided by the European Council at its meeting in Madrid on 15 and 16 December 1995. Apart from the introduction scenario, the Madrid Council decided that the name of the single currency will be the euro.

The introduction scenario consists of three phases (see also the timetable in Appendix One). Phase A starts as early as possible in 1998, when the decision will be taken which member states fulfil the necessary conditions to enter monetary union in 1999. Phase B starts on 1 January 1999, as provided in the Treaty and is the beginning of stage three of EMU. Phase C begins on 1 January 2002 at the latest and will last six months at most. During Phase C, euro banknotes and coins will be introduced and it ends when notes and coins denominated in national currencies cease to be legal tender.

Phase A: who will participate in monetary union?
The changeover scenario for the introduction of the euro is based on 1 January 1999 as the starting date of the third stage of EMU. Before

that, the Council in the composition of heads of state or government, will have to confirm which member states fulfil the necessary conditions for the adoption of a single currency, as laid down in the Treaty on European Union. These conditions include the independence of each member state's national Central Bank and the achievement of a high degree of sustainable convergence of the economies. For the latter, the Treaty specifies four so-called convergence criteria: price stability, sustainability of public finance, the observation of normal fluctuation margins within the Exchange Rate Mechanism (ERM) and the level of long-term interest rates (see Appendix Two). The decision will be based on the data about economic performance of the member states in 1997. As these data become available with a certain delay, such a decision can only be taken at the beginning of 1998. On the other hand, the time needed to assure that all necessary preparations are completed, will require this decision to be taken as early as possible in 1998.

Once the decision has been taken, the heads of state or government of the participating member states will appoint the Executive Board of the European Central Bank (ECB). The ECB will be established, so that it can begin its preparations in order to be ready for conducting monetary policy on 1 January 1999. Also, the production of euro banknotes and coins can start. Moreover, legislation needed for operating monetary policy will have to be adopted.

Phase B: the beginning of monetary union
On 1 January 1999, stage three of EMU will start. It is characterised by the irrevocable fixing of the exchange rates of the participating member states and the euro becoming a currency in its own right. Its external value will be that of the present basket ecu, which will cease to exist. The ECB will start conducting a single monetary policy and national central banks will no longer conduct their own monetary policy; they will merely act as agents for the ECB.

In economic terms, the monetary union will then exist, even though euro notes and coins will only start circulating three years later: exchange rate risk will have been eliminated and there will be a single monetary policy. As the exchange rate risk is currently the main determinant of interest rate differences between member states, these differences will wane. Any remaining interest rate differential will be caused by technical factors, such as market liquidity and differences in credit risk.

In this period, the euro will only exist as book money in the bank accounts. Notes and coins will all be denominated in national currencies. Payments in euros will only be able to be made by bank transfers, cheque, credit card, electronic fund transfers, etc. Any legal obstacle for using the euro will have been removed and anyone will be free to use the euro, but no one will be obliged to do so. This is the so-called 'no compulsion, no prohibition' principle. National notes and coins will continue to remain legal tender within the country of issuance until the completion of the changeover process. See Chapter Eight for a description of the legal framework.

The irrevocability of the exchange rate fixing and monetary union will be ensured in several ways. First, monetary policy will be conducted in euros. This means that the monetary policy operations between the national central banks and the commercial banks will be carried out in euros. A new interbank payment system, called the TARGET system, will be put in place so as to ensure that payment operations between the European System of Central Banks (ESCB) and the banking system can be effected quickly and safely. It will operate in euros. Secondly, new government bond issues will be denominated in euros. Thirdly, as long as different national monetary units exist, they will be legally equivalent to the euro; national currencies will legally be non-decimal expressions of the euro.

Phase C: the introduction of euro notes and coins
By 1 January 2002 at the latest, euro banknotes and coins will start to circulate alongside national notes and coins. During this phase, euro notes and coins as well as national currency notes and coins will have legal tender status, which means that they have to be accepted as a means of payment. National notes and coins will be gradually withdrawn.

At the end of phase C, national notes and coins will lose their legal tender status. This will be on 1 July 2002 at the latest. The Madrid scenario explicitly provides for subsidiarity in this matter, which means that member states can decide to shorten the length of Phase C. The need for shortening phase C could arise from the additional costs of a long dual legal tender situation. Any situation in which two currencies coexist as legal tender will require dual cash handling, dual accounting, dual pricing, etc. It does not only lead to large additional costs, but increases the risk of mistakes and fraud. Many private market participants, in particular the retail sector, object to such a long dual legal tender period. Therefore, many member states are thinking of considerably shortening Phase C. Even a so called 'legal big bang', in which the legal tender status changes overnight, is not excluded. A legal big bang does not mean that the logistics of changing the cash would be done in one day, but it would concentrate the changeover period in a very short space of time. And any acceptance of national currency after the changeover, would be done on a voluntary basis, as a service to the customer.

End of phase C: disappearance of national notes and coins
By definition, phase C ends when national notes and coins lose their legal tender status, which will be on 1 July 2002 at the latest. The changeover process will then be completed: the entire economy will be denominated in euros. It does not, however, imply that national notes and coins will have become valueless: they may still be exchanged free of charge at the national central banks for a certain period. This is common practice when member states are replacing bank notes by new ones.

Member states joining later
Member states that do not fulfil the necessary conditions for the adoption of a single currency at the beginning of 1998, will join monetary union in a later stage. The Treaty provides that at least every two years, or at the request of a member state concerned, the Council shall decide which member states with delayed entrance to monetary union fulfil the necessary conditions to join monetary union. This may be before 2002 and it cannot be ruled out that such a decision could be taken in the course of 1999. Whether in that case it is decided that the member state in question will introduce euro notes and coins in 2002, will depend on the exact date of the decision and the stage of preparation in that member state.

The Madrid European Council determined a clear framework for the introduction of the euro. Since Madrid, many economic agents, especially in the financial sector and in administrations, have started preparations.

The benefits of monetary union will materialise gradually: some will arise with the elimination of exchange rate risks on 1 January 1999; for some other benefits, such as the integration of payment systems, it will take more time to be realised. Also, as more member states join monetary union, benefits will increase, even for those who joined earlier.

Chapter Four

Exchange Rate Stability

THE INTERIM PERIOD

Santiago Fernández de Lis and José Viñals

The interim period is that which elapses between the announcement in the spring of 1998 of the countries participating in Economic and Monetary Union and the irrevocable fixing of their exchange rates at the beginning of Stage Three in January 1999. This period, which spans the final months of Stage Two, is characterised by the risks of instability arising from the co-existence of monetary policies still in the hands of national authorities and market expectations focusing on the final conversion rates. The interim period is also crucial in the process towards EMU because of the various key decisions that have to be taken: from the appointment of the top officials of the European Central Bank, to the adoption of important pieces of legislation concerning the changeover to the single currency and the working of the single monetary policy from the onset of Stage Three.

Effects of the European Council's decision on participating countries

The announcement by the European Council of the countries initially participating in monetary union will hardly be a surprise for financial markets. In the first months of 1998, the macroeconomic performance of EU countries in 1997 will be visible and closely scrutinised by markets, particularly with regard to the selection criteria for EMU. Nevertheless, the Treaty provisions on the convergence criteria give some interpretative leeway to the authorities when deciding which countries are fit to participate in EMU. As a consequence, market expectations of who will be the initial participants will include some element of uncertainty. Except in the cases of countries whose expectation of joining monetary union is either nil or 100%, the announcement will have an impact on the equilibrium exchange rates. But even if the decision is fully anticipated because it is filtered to the public gradually, there will be other effects whose impact will be felt in a gradual fashion and in the period immediately before the formal announcement.

Assuming that markets reasonably expect that the euro will be stronger than the currencies of any of the non-participating states, the participating currencies whose previous probability of qualifying was lower than 100% will appreciate, and conversely, the non-participating currencies whose previous probability was above zero will depreciate. The size of these effects will depend on the previous probability of qualifying assigned to each currency and, in the case of the non-participating countries, also on the kind of monetary, budgetary and exchange rate policies expected to be implemented in subsequent years. It can be argued that for those countries subject to derogation which have previously introduced the institutional changes required to participate in EMU, in particular those concerning central bank independence, and which have showed a good although insufficient convergence pattern, the scenario of temporary non-participation will not incorporate inflationary expectations significantly higher than those of the euro area. If this is the case, the impact of the announcement of non-participation on their exchange rates will not be as significant, although some short-term overreaction of financial markets linked to the frustrated hopes of participation cannot be excluded.

The decision as to which countries participate in EMU from the outset will also be reflected in interest rates. As regards participating countries, their respective long-term interest rate differentials will necessarily be rather narrow before the announcement, due to the existence of an interest rate convergence requirement. Short-term interest rate spreads will be small at first and then tend to disappear in the interim period, eventually leading to a common level at the beginning of Stage Three, although for longer maturities factors like sovereign risk may imply some small differentials. The respective short-term interest rates of potential euro currencies will converge towards lower levels, provided that the markets expect the euro to be at least as strong as the strongest EU currency. The course of interest rates of non-participating countries will, in turn, depend on several factors: the magnitude of the initial depreciating pressures, the design of the framework for monetary and exchange rate cooperation between the included and the temporarily excluded countries (the so-called

ERM 2), and their economic policy reactions. It is likely that some of these countries, facing downward pressures on their exchange rates, might have to resort to interest rate increases as a counter measure.

In addition to the aforementioned reactions of financial markets to the announcement of the countries chosen to participate in EMU from the outset, there are two main sources of potential instability during the interim period. One is linked to the uncertainty over the conversion rates, and another to the possible spillover effects from the non-participating currencies.

Conversion rates

The choice of conversion rates is a key decision when forming the monetary union for readily understandable reasons: these rates will determine the relative value of assets and liabilities of EMU countries, and will influence their competitiveness inside the single market. It is therefore of the utmost importance for the sound functioning of the monetary union that these rates adequately reflect the economic fundamentals of the countries concerned. It is also very important from the viewpoint of markets that these rates are set in line with market rates, and that markets have the possibility of influencing conversion rates and take positions or cover them at each moment in time.

The Treaty establishes in its Article 109l.4 that the adoption of the conversion rates 'shall by itself not modify the external value of the ECU'. This provision, though somewhat ambiguous, was intended to dispel market fears of arbitrariness in the final decision on conversion rates. The most extensive interpretation of this provision is the implication that conversion rates should coincide with market rates at the end of the interim period. As a result, the authorities may want to convey to the markets messages about the exchange rates that they consider to be in line with fundamentals, or even try to guide market rates to the desired levels. In this regard, one possibility is to announce in advance the conversion rates, the specific mechanism or rule to be used in determining them, or the constraints under which they will be established.

As regards the factors which may strategically influence the choice of conversion rates it is important to keep in mind that they can be, to some extent, mutually offsetting, so that it is ultimately not an easy task to determine the net gain, if any, of possible strategies to influence conversion rates in the interim period. Firstly, there may be an incentive to set an artificially depreciated exchange rate to obtain a competitive edge. However, it should be taken into account that this may also entail a loss insofar as the state has a net liability position in foreign currency vis-à-vis other participants in EMU. Furthermore, any attempt to set an artificially depreciated exchange rate would be discouraged by the risk that other countries might try to follow a similar strategy, leading to a futile succession of competitive devaluations. Finally, any depreciation of a participating currency during the interim period would exert domestic pressures on the prices of non-traded goods in Stage Three once the parities have been irrevocably locked. In any case, sizable exchange rate movements during or at the end of the interim period would be at odds with progress towards monetary union.

Relationships between future EMU participants and non-participants during the interim period

As mentioned earlier, the decision on which states are the founding members of EMU will probably have an impact on exchange rates. As a simplifying assumption, suppose that the currencies of the states joining EMU tend to appreciate vis-à-vis the non-participating currencies. Given the high degree of commercial and financial integration among EU countries, the depreciation of the non-participating currencies will have an impact on the euro area currencies. This effect would be asymmetric due to the likely different degree of commercial and financial links of each participating state with respect to the states with a derogation. The magnitude of this effect will mainly depend on the size of the initial monetary union: the smaller the number of selected countries, the greater the destabilising effect of the countries with a derogation. On the contrary, under a relatively wide initial EMU, the risk of exchange rate pressures arising from the non-participating countries would be relatively minor. The timing of the establishment and the specific nature of the new ERM are very important in this regard.

Relative importance of the sources of uncertainty

As can be seen in Charts One to Three, the relative importance of the risks described above will probably evolve during the interim period. Indeed, the uncertainty associated with the final conversion rates in the absence of any kind of preannouncement by the authorities will increase steadily before and during this period. In contrast, the uncertainty over the choice of the participating currencies will be highest in the period immediately before the decision by the European Council. Once the selection has been made, uncertainty will be re-directed towards the likely instability of the non-participant exchange rates. That instability, in turn, is likely to decrease slowly as the interim period progresses.

It is interesting to see how these sources of uncertainty may be affected by the configuration of EMU. Chart One describes the basic scenario corresponding to overall market expectations at present. Charts Two and Three show the evolution of both types of uncertainty under the alternative scenarios of a relatively wide and a relatively narrow EMU, respectively, compared with the basic reference scenario illustrated in the first chart. A wide EMU will imply higher uncertainty concerning conversion rates because some currencies would probably have experienced a higher volatility in the previous period, and also because market views on their equilibrium exchange rates will probably be less focused; on the other hand, if EMU is relatively wide, the effect of non-participating currencies will logically be small. A narrow EMU will show the opposite characteristics: the uncertainty over the conversion rates will be relatively small, but the

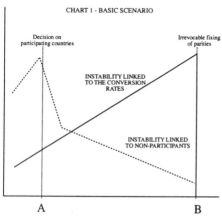

CHART 1 - BASIC SCENARIO

Decision on participating countries

Irrevocable fixing of parities

INSTABILITY LINKED TO THE CONVERSION RATES

INSTABILITY LINKED TO NON-PARTICIPANTS

A   B

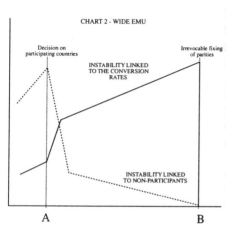

CHART 2 - WIDE EMU

Decision on participating countries

Irrevocable fixing of parities

INSTABILITY LINKED TO THE CONVERSION RATES

INSTABILITY LINKED TO NON-PARTICIPANTS

A   B

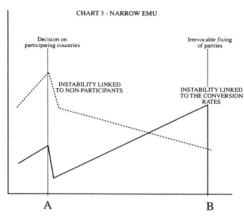

CHART 3 - NARROW EMU

Decision on participating countries

Irrevocable fixing of parities

INSTABILITY LINKED TO NON-PARTICIPANTS

INSTABILITY LINKED TO THE CONVERSION RATES

A

B

destabilising impact of non-participants will be stronger. It is extremely difficult to assess the net impact of both effects on the total risks during the interim period.

It is important to keep in mind that this analysis of the sources of uncertainty and their likely evolution during the interim period has been made without taking into account the potential policy reactions of the authorities to counteract such uncertainty. The authorities obviously might adopt policies to mitigate the destabilising effect of the factors mentioned above. In particular, as has been said before, a pre-announcement by the authorities may stabilise market expectations regarding conversion rates, and a reinforcement of the ERM instruments may reduce the risks of instability arising from non-participating currencies. If the authorities adopt such policies, both types of instability showed in the charts may be substantially reduced.

Apart from the two types of uncertainties described above, during this period there will be the risk of instability as a consequence of political or economic shocks. Among the first type of shocks one may imagine the usual uncertainty linked to elections and referenda which will have a particularly destabilising impact in this period, especially if EMU is an issue in political campaigns and if there are political parties of some influence opposing monetary union. Economic (asymmetric) shocks, however, are not very likely in such a short period.

The need to coordinate monetary policies during the interim period

The risks of instability during the interim period exist but should not be overstated. The countries eligible for monetary union will have reached at this stage a very high degree of convergence which will be reinforced by the strong commitment to establish a single currency in a very short time. Moreover, several elements which will be in place in this period are expected to contribute to the credibility of the final steps towards EMU. Firstly, the ERM mechanisms will continue to exist, and may enhance the coordination of monetary policies. Secondly, the European Central Bank will be up and running, and this should help reinforce the common decision-making process of EMU countries. And finally, other institutional aspects of monetary union which are as yet insufficiently defined will be specified in the interim period, and this will foster confidence among the public, and in particular the financial markets, in EMU.

To conclude, the decisions during the interim period about which states will participate in EMU from the outset and the final conversion rates are significant sources of uncertainty. Undoubtedly, there is always the danger that these uncertainties will translate into market instabilities. Nevertheless, if the economic policies of both participating and non-participating currencies are sound and if an appropriate ERM 2 is set up, it is reasonable to expect that market instability will be minimised.

PHASE A

Pierre Valentin

In the first half of 1998, the European Council will select the countries they consider worthy of joining the single currency. At the latest on 1 January 1999, bilateral parities will be irrevocably fixed and so will be the parity of the ecu (whose name will be changed to the euro) against participating currencies. For the time being, market participants have no other official information about the way the forex market will be managed during this period which starts with the conception and ends with the birth of the single currency, a period of nine months called Phase A.

Participating currencies
How and when will the bilateral parities be fixed? The Maastricht Treaty says (Article 109l.4) that the conversion rates must be voted on unanimously by participating member states, on the day the single currency is created. In the same article, the continuity of the external value of the ecu in this process is assured.

The required unanimity means that a currency's level purely determined by the market on one particular day, which could appear unfair to a participating country, may not be accepted. On the other hand, why change bilateral parities which have been required by the Treaty to stay stable for at least two years?

These two constraints give a high probability to the following: either the bilateral parities will be announced some time in advance of January 1999 or they will be the result of a formula which will be announced some time in advance of January 1999. Without shocks, there will be a clear understanding of the bilateral parities before the single currency is created, which will allow market exchange rates to converge towards their definitive values.

Amongst the ideas which have been mooted to ensure a well-ordered transition, is the proposal of using an average value (over a certain period of time) of bilateral exchange rates to fix the currencies of participating countries. The idea is appealing because the more time passes, the less uncertain, and hence volatile, the parity is. [1] With that kind of method, there would be, apart from unpredictable events which could derail EMU during Phase A, a very low volatility of exchange rates.

But what about short term rates? Let us assume that a country whose rates are 5.5% (not far from Irish rates at the time of writing) is selected along with a country whose rates are 3% (German rates at the same time). If, in March 1998, these two countries are selected for EMU, and if the bilateral parity is the average value of the exchange rate from March 1998 to the end of December 1998, there will be an obvious arbitrage: buy every day the same amount of the high yielding currency, financed in the low yielding one until the last day of December 1998. As the average value will be equal to the conversion value, it will be equal to the value of the last day. Therefore the profit of the arbitrage will be the average carry of the position.

The ecu
The transition to the single currency will have important consequences for other markets, especially the ecu market. The ecu is a basket currency, which is also traded on the foreign exchange markets. Its value on the foreign exchange markets (the actual value) often differs from its theoretical value, which can be derived from the value of its components.

The divergence between the actual value of the ecu in the forex market and the theoretical value has been very volatile in recent years, fluctuating from -3% and more to -0.30%. The key role played by brokers in this market will probably continue to be important up to the last trading day of 1998. The divergence will be zero exactly at the time currencies are fixed, because at that time, 1 ecu-basket = 1 euro and 1 ecu-market = 1 euro (continuity of contracts, hence of deposits). But, in order to unwind their positions, brokers who are long in the market ecu against the component currencies (or short if the divergence has changed from the current discount to premium) will need to buy or sell non-participating currencies against ecus exactly at the price that will have been used to fix the conversion rate of the ecu-euro. Assuming the fixing is done when markets are closed, one can expect a very active and nervous market on the day before, for the ecu as well as non-participating currencies.

The size of this possible effect depends on the weight of non-participating currencies. In order to fix orders of magnitude, assume that 25% of the basket does not participate in the single currency. If the overnight fluctuation of these currencies is 0.4%, a residual discount or premium of 0.1% will be impossible to reduce. This would not be a problem. Nevertheless, the big flows due to unwinding need to be closely followed, and one cannot rule out the necessity of central bank action in these markets.

Even if the averaging period starts before March 1998, it is difficult to avoid consequences of this process on monetary policies in 1998. Moreover, the effect of the arbitrage would be to continuously push up the high yielding currency, which could bring about an unrealistic bilateral parity or force large interventions from central banks. So averaging needs strong cooperation, not to say an arithmetical determination, of relative monetary policies.

One of the simplest ways to obtain this is to have the same short term interest rates in participating countries in March 1998: this implies using an average either starting or coinciding with the current exchange rate in March. In this case, an interesting conclusion is that the convergence on short rates could be much quicker and profitable than the convergence in ten year bond yields which has been the most fashionable until recently. Another idea is to announce the bilateral parities which will have been agreed by the heads of state or government of the EU in advance of January 1999. The main question is when? If the announcement is made too early and if some event occurs thereafter which could alter the competitiveness or the price of assets in one country, the necessary change will be impossible. On the other hand, if the exchange rates have not been announced at the same time as the selection of countries, markets could be very nervous, speculating on secret targets even if they do not exist. Once the rates are announced, the forward exchange rate of any participating currency against any other one will be known and perfectly stable as long the EMU process is credible. That means exchange rate volatility would be reduced to almost zero, but creeping up if an event able to derail EMU occurs.

Non-participating currencies

A potential source of volatility is located at the beginning of phase A. Before the selection of countries is made, three kinds of countries will probably be identified by the market: almost certain participants, definite non-participants and uncertain. Countries in the third group will have inflation, or budget deficits very close to the Maastricht criteria but not fulfilling them unequivocally. Although preparatory reports will be released by the EMI and the Commission, the suspense for these countries is likely to last until the meeting of the European Council, since markets may fear that decision will involve a certain amount of bargaining between member states. If, for these countries the market has priced a 50% probability of EMU membership, then, just after the decision is made, it will have to move interest rate spreads and probably exchange rates (at least exchange rates volatilities) to levels compatible with the new situation: either membership or exclusion. It is unlikely that this substantial adjustment of the market can be avoided. Europe has been used to this kind of situation in recent years, with a lot of events where the date is known and the impact on the market can be reasonably estimated, but the outcome is largely unpredictable, such as elections and referendums. Usually the volatility is very high before these events and continuously increasing, because all the uncertainty is concentrated on one day. After the event, volatility decreases markedly after the sharp move of the market.

Non-European currencies

Last, the stability, or instability, of European currencies vis-à-vis the US dollar during phase A is worth some analysis. Some studies already published have tried to estimate the impact of EMU on currency allocation of big financial institutions, especially Central Banks. A lot of factors at work will favour purchase of euros: underweighting of European currencies in non-European central bank reserves, increased use of euros as an invoicing currency, the level of non-EU currencies reserves (including gold) of EMU central banks which is already huge. Against that, some factors will help the other currencies, especially in phase A: the diversification effect will push European investors out of EMU, especially if convergence trades are made still more credible by the very existence of EMU.

European Central Banks, which hold sizeable amounts of DM in their reserves (this is probably the case for the 'hard core' countries) will wish to bring non-euro currencies to the ECB's reserves. Finally, in many member states, governments, not central banks, manage the currency reserves. First, they will try to avoid destabilising forex markets and pushing already expensive currencies higher. Second, they are keen to extract profits from their central bank in order to reduce their budget deficit, which is possible only by achieving capital gains on currencies; and it is not certain that the dollar's value in central banks' books is much lower than its current level.

Certain market commentators suggest that the number of countries in the single currency could also play a role: if many countries join the monetary union in 1999, this could imply softer criteria, and thus a weaker euro.

A process which aims to fix exchange rates definitively may at first destabilise them: a trend evident since the ratification of the Maastricht Treaty and which could still be valid in years to come. Nevertheless, it seems that potential volatility in forex markets will be localised at the beginning of Phase A, and focus on non-participating currencies.

---

[1] Note that this implies the use of a reference currency, (for instance the DM) against which the others are quoted: indeed, the average of the French franc denominated in DM is not the inverse of the average of the Deutsche mark denominated in FFr.

Chapter Five

Monetary Policy: targets, instruments and changeover problems

Christian Pfister

The European System of Central Banks

As early as possible in the first half of 1998, the European Central Bank will be created and located in Frankfurt. The ESCB will be made up of the ECB and the national central banks of the participating member states. However, the member states will retain sole responsibility for the conduct of their monetary policies until the ECB starts operating on 1 January 1999. The reason for creating the ECB before that date is to give it time to finalise the strategy and put in place the instruments of the single monetary policy.

The decision-making bodies of the ECB will be the governing council and the executive board. The governing council will comprise the members of the executive board and the governors of the national central banks. It will act by a simple majority with each member having one vote and the president the casting vote. The proceedings of the meetings will be confidential, unless the governing council decides otherwise; and it will meet at least ten times a year. It will formulate the single monetary policy including, as appropriate, decisions relating to intermediate monetary objectives and key interest rates.

The executive board will comprise the president and the vice-president of the ECB and four other members. All members will be appointed by the heads of state or government of the monetary union, on recommendation of the Council of economic and finance ministers (Ecofin), after consultation with the European Parliament and the governing council of the ECB. Their term of office will be eight years and not renewable. The executive board will implement monetary policy in accordance with the guidelines laid down by the governing council.

Basic principles of the single monetary policy

The basic principles of the single monetary policy are laid down in the Treaty. They are :

- its primary objective will be to maintain price stability; without prejudice to that objective, the ESCB will support the general economic policies of the Union;

- the ESCB will have to act in accordance with the principle of an open market economy with free competition. This principle can be understood as prohibiting the ESCB from having recourse to so-called direct control instruments such as authority limits to credit expansion or capital control measures. It also has a bearing on the definition of the single monetary policy instruments and procedures;

- the ESCB will be independent, at the level of both the ECB and the national central banks;

- the ESCB will be accountable; the president of Ecofin and a Commissioner will have the right to attend the meetings of the governing council, without voting rights. Symmetrically, the president of the ECB will be invited to meetings of Ecofin when the latter discusses issues touching upon the objectives and missions of the ESCB, such as exchange rate issues. Finally, the ECB will report annually on the monetary policy of both the previous and the current year;

- the ESCB will be prohibited from granting credit to public bodies or subscribing to securities issued by them; of course, this does not preclude the refinancing of publicly-owned credit institutions, the purchase of public securities in the secondary market or their use as collateral in refinancing operations.

Based on the Treaty principles for monetary policy, the European Monetary Institute is preparing the monetary policy instruments for the ECB:

- monetary policy decisions will be taken centrally by the ECB but, in line with the principle of subsidiarity, policy will be implemented in a decentralised manner by the national central banks; this implies a very high degree of harmonisation in the instruments and procedures used by the central banks in order to preserve a single monetary policy stance;

- there will be a single monetary stance, defined as the equality of interest rate levels in the interbank market throughout the euro area. This also requires a very high degree of harmonisation of instruments and procedures as well as the possibility of arbitraging within the monetary union. This possibility will be offered as the TARGET (Trans-European Automated Real Time Gross Settlement Express Transfer) system, that will link the Real Time Gross Settlement systems operated in each country of the euro area, and allow same-day value transfers;

- the single monetary policy, as well as the foreign exchange policy, will be implemented in euros from the start of the ESCB operations. To facilitate that implementation, new public debt issues will be denominated in euros (some governments have already announced that they will immediately convert the stock of public debt) and payment systems will have to allow for the good functioning of a money market based on the euro. However, national central banks will be allowed to offer conversion facilities between the euro and national denominations to commercial banks that would not be able to equip themselves with such facilities.

Possible strategies for the single monetary policy

Among possible strategies for the single monetary policy, some are likely to be rejected by the ECB. Such strategies include the targeting of an interest or exchange rate objective, of the growth rate of nominal GDP and of the monetary base.

The choice of an interest rate objective is unlikely both because it is difficult for central banks to influence long-term interest rates in a predictable manner, inter alia because they are affected by fiscal policies and external developments, and because targeting a short-term interest rate may lead the ESCB to reacting too little and too late to comply with its final objective of price stability. Of course, this does not preclude recourse to a short-term money market rate as an operational target for the implementation of monetary policy.

An exchange rate objective may also not be fully consistent with the commitment to price stability as the euro area is likely to be less open than most participating countries. As a consequence, keeping the exchange rate of the euro stable may be compatible with some deviations from price stability at least in the short run. Moreover, the ESCB will not have full responsibility in determining the exchange rate policy of the monetary union, and the euro will play the anchoring role in the monetary arrangement with the currencies of those countries not participating in the euro area from the outset.

Targeting a growth rate for nominal GDP would not be easily achievable as monetary policy can influence the evolution of nominal income only with lags. It could also create uncertainty about the level of inflation in the short run and the responsibility of the ESCB in that regard.

Finally, targeting the monetary base would have the advantage of concentrating on a variable which is under the full control of the central bank. However, money supply multipliers have displayed instability in the past and such a strategy may entail a high volatility of short-term interest rates and more generally of financial markets.

Monetary targeting and inflation targeting
The main advantage of a monetary targeting strategy is that for the past twenty years it has been the strategy employed by the Bundesbank, the central bank with the best track record of fighting inflation in Western Europe, and whose currency has de facto provided the anchor of the Exchange Rate Mechanism. By adopting this strategy, the ESCB would put itself in a position to inherit the credibility of the Bundesbank. Among other advantages, monetary aggregates are normally more directly under the control of the central bank than other economic variables and empirical research has so far shown that such aggregates exhibit a fairly good level of stability at the EU level. However, the current performance of EU-wide monetary aggregates may be attributable to a rather slow pace of financial innovation in some member states, including Germany, and the regime shift implied by EMU may in itself be the source of some changes in empirical relationships.

Inflation targeting has the advantage of being directly linked to the final objective of the ESCB. This strategy has been used with some success by several countries in the EU, including the United Kingdom. However, it was only adopted recently and its implementation has so far taken place in a context conducive to low inflation, that of slow growth and declining worldwide inflation. In addition, there may be a risk that economic agents remain more sensitive after the beginning of monetary union to inflationary developments at the domestic level rather than at the euro area level, making this strategy less transparent.

In any case, one should not overemphasise the difference between monetary targeting and inflation targeting as both strategies can be seen as compatible with the final objective of the ESCB and its independent status. Furthermore, it is worth noting that in practice central banks following one strategy or the other also monitor a broad range of economic and financial indicators when they have to take policy decisions.

The instruments and procedures of the single monetary policy
In December 1995, the EMI Council agreed to undertake preparatory work on all technical and institutional issues relating to a basic set of monetary policy instruments, consisting of two standing facilities and several open market instruments. In keeping with Article 19 of its Statute, reserve requirements will also be available to the ESCB, although there is not yet a consensus between national central banks on whether they should actually be employed. Issues related to monetary policy procedures are under review at the EMI as well as in the central banks.

Standing facilities are accessible at the discretion of central bank counterparties. They are used by central banks to set a corridor for short-term market rates, thereby limiting their volatility, as well as to signal the medium-term orientation of monetary policy. There could be two such facilities:

- a marginal lending facility that would set the higher limit for market rates, although there is not yet agreement on the maturity of this facility, it could be available at 24 hours, as is presently the case for the Bundesbank's Lombard facility. As a consequence, it could also play the role of an end-of-day facility in order to finance any end-of-day overdrafts that commercial banks may have on their accounts with the central bank when the money market is closed and that would have to be collateralised;

- a deposit facility that would set the lower limit for market rates when there is excess liquidity on that market. It is generally agreed that, to this end, a deposit facility would be more in line with market principles than a refinancing facility at below market rate, like the discount facility currently used in Austria, Germany or Italy, access to which has to be rationed by the central bank in order to limit the amount of liquidity provided through it.

Open market operations

Open market operations are used at the discretion of the central bank. As is currently the case in most EU countries, open market operations should be the main channel through which liquidity is either supplied to the market or withdrawn from it. This is because they are flexible, efficient in the steering of money market rates, respectful of market procedures for the allocation of liquidity and may also play a signalling function.

Among these operations, the conduct of regular reverse operations (repurchase agreements or collateralised loans), either at variable rate or at fixed rate if their signalling role is to be reinforced, is likely to be used in order to provide the bulk of refinancing.

A range of fine tuning instruments should also be available to the ESCB. They could include quick tender transactions, that is, reverse transactions that can be held with same-day value in order to accommodate liquidity shocks, but also outright transactions, foreign exchange swaps, the issuance of central bank paper and the collection of fixed-term deposits.

Reserve requirements

Two functions are usually assigned to reserve requirements: contributing to monetary control and helping to manage the money market.

When required reserves are not remunerated or less than fully remunerated, they increase the negative elasticity of money demand as commercial banks pass on their cost to their customers, thereby diminishing the attractiveness and level of bank deposits. However, there are certainly limits to such a use of reserve requirements, which can be conducive to delocation and disintermediation of financial activity. In that regard, reserve requirement ratios have been lowered in several major industrialised countries, including Canada, France, Germany, Italy, Japan and the United States, in recent years.

Reserve requirements also help manage the money market by enlarging the demand for central bank money and, when combined with averaging provisions, the maintenance of minimum reserve balances on average over a certain period of time, usually a month, by stabilising money market rates. The latter function is performed because requirements are fulfilled in relation with commercial bank expectations about market rate changes in the remainder of the maintenance period. It is also performed irrespectively of whether required reserves are remunerated or not, as long as they are not remunerated at market rates.

Procedures

As regards procedures, one major implication of conformity with market principles will be to ensure equal treatment of financial institutions to ESCB monetary policy operations. Furthermore, possible discontinuities with current practices should be minimised in order to take account of specific features of national financial markets and banking systems. Issues still under discussion at the EMI and in national central banks include the definition of the ranges of counterparties and collaterals.

Concerning the range of counterparties, it is generally expected that it should be relatively broad in the case of standing facilities, regular open market operations and outright transactions in order to ensure equal treatment, a widespread distribution of liquidity throughout the monetary union and an effective decentralisation in the execution of the single monetary policy. For some fine tuning operations such as quick tenders and foreign exchange swaps, however, considerations of operational efficiency would a priori require limits in the number of counterparties.

Article 18 of the ESCB statute requires it to base its open market and credit operations on adequate collateral. In order to ensure harmonisation of ESCB procedures, to avoid discrimination of holders and issuers of debt instruments and to guarantee continuity, it has been envisaged to make a distinction between two categories of debt instruments accepted as collateral. A first list (tier one), selected by the ECB, could include debt instruments that are marketable, liquid and centrally deposited. In order to ensure continuity; a second list (tier two), consisting of additional instruments whether marketable or not, could be established by national central banks under their own responsibility but in the context of guidelines formulated by the ECB. Tier two instruments could for example include private paper such as those now accepted by the Banque de France or trade bills currently discounted by the Bundesbank.

Chapter Six

The Financial Markets after January 1999

Graham Bishop

The changeover scenario agreed at the 1995 Madrid summit, together with decisions already made by the European Monetary Institute, have set some important guidelines for the changeover of the financial markets:

> Foreign exchange and money market activities of the European Central Bank will be conducted in euros from the beginning of Stage Three of EMU. As the central bank plays a pivotal role in the money markets and the money and foreign exchange markets are really only two sides of the same coin, this decision effectively means that all these markets will convert to euros on the first day. Market participants accept this and are planning accordingly.

> All new 'tradable' government debt issued after January 1999 will be in euros. This decision papered over the debate about whether the entire stock of outstanding government debt should be converted at the outset. However, the French and Belgian governments have announced already that they will redenominate all their debt immediately. The debate on this issue is very active across the EU and it would not be surprising to see a wave of announcements by other governments in the coming months about an immediate changeover. The signalling effect of such official decisions will be very important, both because of the relative size of government debt markets and also the message that the private sector will take about how it should arrange its affairs, if it is not to find itself at a disadvantage.

The direct consequences of these decisions are being analysed by a variety of market participants and the ripples are spreading out rapidly. The changeover is also seen as a golden opportunity to reform Europe's financial markets so that they do turn into a single, and technologically sophisticated, system. Initially work focused on legal questions relating to the continuity of contracts. The regulations (see Chapter Eight) have been designed in close consultation with market participants and appear to fulfil all the needs. Currently, the main focus is the government bond markets with swaps and equities some way behind.

Equities are seen as presenting relatively few conversion problems because the markets themselves can choose the currency in which they trade shares. The companies will choose when they convert their own operations and presumably will follow that through with dividend declarations and payments in euros. Conceptually, the conversion of the par value of shares should have no impact on their market price.

The problems of the *swap* markets are being analysed thoroughly by the International Swap Dealers Association and the passage of the legal regulation on the euro should clear away many problems. A key question is the transition to new reference rates for floating interest rates. If a swap contract refers to PIBOR and that is converted into EuroIBOR with a different panel of reference banks, could there be a difference in the rate because of the new composition?

The relative size of the *Government Bond Markets*, and the signalling effect of official actions, means that they are the key market. Two sets of issues have emerged:

> *Re-denomination and liquidity improvement.* While discussing redenomination, Treasury officials are also considering steps to improve the liquidity of their issues so as to minimise any spread between their bonds and whatever the markets set as the benchmark. In many cases, discussion focuses on creating single issues which can be tapped regularly until they build up to a size which is manifestly liquid. This may include conversion offers to start a new line of fungible securities.

> *Standardisation of market conventions.* Market conventions can be split into two categories, essential and optional. The essential category would include standardisation of day counts for interest calculation; annual or semi annual coupon frequency

and price quotation in decimals, rather than in fractions or by yield. The argument for decimal pricing seem clear-cut but the balance of the debate on the other issues is not decisive.

The capital markets are beginning to realise that there is much to be done in the remaining 500 or so business days to January 1999. By the end of Phase C (at the latest, mid 2002) any teething problems should have been overcome and the euromarkets should be developing rapidly as the world's largest government bond market. The table below shows the relative scale of the equity and bond markets, with the tradable sector of the latter shown separately.

The Euromarket

Trillions of ecus, as at October 1996

	Tradable government bonds	Bonds total publicly issued	Equities
EU ecu (equiv.)	2.2	5.5	2.0
US dollar	1.7	7.0	4.5
Japanese yen	1.0	3.0	1.4
of which:			
Deutschmark	0.5	1.8	0.3
Italian lira	0.3	0.9	0.1
French franc	0.4	0.8	0.2
UK sterling	0.3	0.4	1.0

1 Fixed rate, over one year life remaining.
2 End 1995.
3 Based on the proportion of market capitalisation which is available to investors.

Sources: Salomon Brothers Inc World Government Bond Index, Salomon Brothers Inc World Equity Index, 'How Big is the World Bond Market? 1996 Update'.

The development of a pan-European market on this scale and in a single currency should act as a magnet for global savings and enable Europe to achieve the lowest interest rates consistent with economic fundamentals. It should also spawn a full range of financial products to match the scale of those that exist in the dollar markets. That would include a market for bonds collateralised by assets such as mortgages, credit card receivables, and so on. Bonds issued by smaller corporations could be issued on the basis of a credit rating, rather than local name recognition. There could be niche markets for riskier securities, perhaps opening the way for states that wish to join the EU to promote the use of the euro in parallel with their own currencies. That should pave the way for European companies and consumers to have access to a wider range of finance than they do today. Correspondingly, savers will be faced with new opportunities to improve the return on their assets.

The foundation of modern fixed-income markets is a liquid market in the bonds of the highest quality creditor, usually central government. Though hardly a source of pride, the tradable government bond markets of the EU comfortably exceed that of the US government. However, European non-government markets are much less developed: in Europe, total bonds outstanding are little more than twice the size of the government market whereas dollar bonds are four times larger than that of the government alone. The relative size of the tradable equity markets also reflects the lower importance of securities markets in Europe.

If Europe's securities markets acquire the same relative importance as US markets, then a prolonged period of expansion lies ahead. Moreover the channels of delivering these products are likely to change to reflect the ability of intermediaries to utilise the single market's 'passport' to offer cross-border services. In combination with potential technological developments, such as Internet dealing, EU financial markets are likely to undergo dramatic changes, triggered by EMU but reflecting other forces as well.

Chapter Seven

Exchange Rate Relations between Ins and Pre-Ins

Salvatore Rebecchini

Not all member states will participate in monetary union in 1999. But those states with a derogation will have to have a stable exchange rate with the euro. This chapter describes the proposed relationship between the ins and the pre-ins.

Orderly exchange rate relationships between countries that will participate in the single currency from its inception (euro area member states) and countries that will not (non-euro area member states) are crucial for strengthening economic and monetary integration in Europe. First, excessive exchange rates fluctuations in the area could cause competitive misalignments and hamper the functioning of the single market. Second, it is in the best interests of non-euro member states that their convergence process continues and is not jeopardised by unwarranted exchange rate fluctuations and speculative attacks.

For all EU countries, orderly exchange rate relations are important to ensure a level playing field for the development of trade and for economic growth. Moreover, for those countries that will remain outside the single currency because they are unable to qualify (technically: member states with a derogation), the existence of a cooperative framework for exchange rate policy will help to sustain and enhance convergence and eventually their accession to the single currency. For countries that will remain outside because they decide to do so — an option available only for the UK and Denmark (the opt-out countries) — a framework for exchange rate cooperation will also be useful to coordinate monetary policy and facilitate the achievement of domestic price stability.

A formal arrangement for exchange rate relations between euro and non-euro area member states is also required to ensure equal treatment among first wave participants of the single currency and latecomers. In fact, Article 109k.2 of the Maastricht Treaty requires the repetition, at least once every two years or at the request of a state with a derogation, of the procedure for determining the participation of new members in the single currency. If a state meets the convergence criteria, including the one requiring the 'observance of the normal fluctuation margins provided for by the exchange rate mechanism of the European Monetary System, for at least two years' (Article 109j.1), the derogation is abrogated and the country can adopt the euro as its domestic currency. Hence it follows that there has to be a technical successor to the European Monetary System (EMS) in order to enable a country with a derogation to respect 'the normal fluctuation margins' and to qualify for the single currency.

With these considerations in mind, policy makers in the relevant bodies, the EU Monetary Committee and the European Monetary Institute, have set out to specify the most appropriate framework for organising exchange rate relations between the euro and non-euro member states, in the interest of all EU members, in accordance with the spirit of Article 109m of the Treaty, which states that 'each Member State shall treat its exchange rate as a matter of common interest'.

Preliminary deliberations on the issue have been endorsed by the European Council in Florence, 21-22 June 1996, which established that a new Exchange Rate Mechanism should replace the present ERM as from the start of stage three. Membership will continue to be voluntary, but non-euro area member states with a derogation are expected to join the mechanism.

The specific details of the new arrangement are yet to be worked out. They will be designed to take into account the following needs that have been identified in the course of the preliminary negotiations: to safeguard the statutory provision for the ECB to maintain price stability; to establish the euro as the anchor for monetary and exchange rate policy cooperation in the area; to accommodate with flexibility the varying degree of economic convergence of the non-euro area member countries; to ensure continuity and equality of treatment with respect to the exchange rate convergence criterion.

It is likely the new arrangement will be characterised by the following features: it will be based on central rates defined with respect to the euro for each non-euro currency — the so called 'hubs and spokes' model — which has the advantage of clearly highlighting the objective of convergence towards the standards of economic performance set by the euro-area. One drawback of such a model is that the maximum fluctuation allowed between two non-euro area currencies would be double that between the euro and any non-euro currency. To counter this problem, it is envisaged that non-euro area members may voluntarily establish bilateral fluctuation bands between their currencies.

It can be expected that the fluctuation band will be relatively wide, similar to the present EMS band (+/- 15%). The argument in favour of maintaining a rather large band is that it has proved effective in the EMS in deterring speculation by establishing a 'two way risk'. It should be able to accommodate the varying degree of convergence that are likely to characterise the group of non-euro area member countries in stage three.

In order to strengthen its credibility and highlight its cooperative nature, the new arrangement should retain the provisions for unlimited and automatic intervention at the margins available in the present EMS. In the same vein the Very Short Term Financing facility of the EMS, utilised for financing intervention, should also be continued.

Within the standard wide band arrangement, non-euro area member countries will have the possibility to establish individually forms of closer exchange rate cooperation with the ECB. The precise content of such arrangements is likely to be left to the negotiation between the parties involved, as it will have to be tailored to the degree of convergence achieved by the country concerned. On the basis of the experience gathered in the wide band EMS, set-ups for closer exchange rate cooperation are likely to cover formal arrangements with narrow bands and automatic intervention to informal target zones.

Finally, to avoid the misalignments of exchange rate parities that in some cases have hampered the EMS, the sustainability of exchange rate relations will need to be closely monitored and the parities realigned in a timely way. It cannot be ruled out that specific procedures to this avail will be included in the new arrangement.

PART TWO: TECHNICAL ASPECTS

Chapter Eight

Legal Aspects

Sammy van Tuyll

The legal framework is a crucial determinant in agents' decision making. This is true for economic activity in general, but particularly so for the introduction of the euro. Thus the legal status of the euro, in particular in the transition period, will to a large extent determine the individual timing of the changeover.

The basis for the legal framework is of course the Treaty. However, some provisions of the Treaty need clarification or further specification in secondary legislation. The sooner these issues are clarified, the better focused preparations can be. This is why the Madrid European Council asked for the technical preparatory work for a Council regulation providing the legal framework for the use of the euro to be completed at the latest by the end of 1996.

There will in fact be two Council regulations. One regulation, called 'Council Regulation on the Introduction of the Euro', will be based on Article 109l.4 of the Treaty. This article provides that the Council shall 'acting with the unanimity of the Member States without a derogation ... take the other measures necessary for the rapid introduction of ... the single currency of those Member States'. Those member states will only be known in early 1998. For convenience, the regulation based on Article 109l.4 will be called Regulation A in this chapter.

The other Council regulation, called 'Council Regulation on Some Provisions Relating to the Introduction of the Euro' will contain those provisions urgently needed for legal certainty, in particular those on the continuity of contracts and on rounding. It will be based on Article 235 of the Treaty, which allows for the adoption of measures to obtain the objectives of the Treaty for which the Treaty has not otherwise provided the necessary powers. Here it will be called Regulation B.

On 16 October 1996, the Commission agreed on the proposals to be submitted to the Council.[1] These proposals, prepared in close collaboration with the European Monetary Institute and with the member states, were discussed by the Council with the aim of reaching agreement at the Dublin European Council meeting in December 1996. Regulation B, the proposal based on Article 235, can then be formally adopted. Once political agreement has been reached on Regulation A, the Article 109l.4 proposal, its statutory adoption in 1998 will be a mere formality.

As a draft of these proposals has already been discussed at length with member state representatives, no major changes are expected. This chapter is based on the Commission proposal and on the general consensus about the ideas expressed in it.

Monetary law

Before dealing with the legal framework in general, an explanation is needed of the specific characteristics of monetary law. The status of a country's currency is governed by monetary law. It determines issues such as the name and the denomination of a currency, its subdivision, and so on. The monetary law of a state is in principle universally recognised: if any given country wishes to change the denomination of its currency, all sums expressed in that country's currency are affected. For instance, France introduced the new franc in 1960, whose value was one hundred times the old franc, so that all amounts expressed in francs had to be divided by a hundred. For someone holding a debt instrument of, say, one million old francs, it would not have been possible to demand payment of the same amount in new francs, irrespective of whether the debt was held inside or outside France. This aspect of monetary law is important, because it entails that the provisions of the Treaty and of the legal framework for the euro that are part of the monetary law, should be recognised worldwide.

Currencies in Phase B

The most important provision of the legal framework is that on 1 January 1999, the euro will become the currency of the member states participating in the monetary union.[2] This is the legal translation of the economic reality that monetary union starts on 1 January 1999 and conversion rates are irrevocably fixed. It meets the Treaty's requirement that the euro will become a currency in its own right at the starting date of the third stage. The euro will be divided into one hundred cents.

On 1 January 1999, the national currencies of the participating member states will become non-decimal subdivisions of the euro. They will continue to exist as subdivisions of the euro until the end of the transitional period, which will be 31 December 2001 at the latest. During this period it will still be possible to calculate price and pay in national currencies, even though they will legally be the euro. Thus if one has a BEF 100 note in one's pocket, it will legally be something like euro 2.51926609, even though the note can be used to pay a debt of 100 BEF.[3] Any contract that was expressed in national currencies before 1 January 1999 will remain so until the end of the transitional period, unless the parties agree to change its denomination. Thus an agreement to pay PTE 1000 on 31 December 1998 will turn into an agreement to pay the corresponding amount in euros converted at the official conversion rates on 1 January 1999, but denominated still as PTE 1000.

In short, there will be contracts denominated in euro units and contracts denominated in national currency units, and of course the existing subdivisions thereof. Legally they will all be expressed in a subdivision of the euro. Though perhaps legally complicated, in practice people will generally keep counting in national currencies until the end of the transitional period, unless they explicitly decide to use the euro denomination. During the transitional period the 'no compulsion, no prohibition' rule will apply: no one will be forced to use the euro-denominated euro, but no one will be prevented from doing so either. As two parties are needed to agree on a contract, the euro-denominated euro can only be used if both parties explicitly agree to do so. This is in particular the case for existing long-term contracts, such as rent and employment contracts. In new contracts there is of course the freedom to agree any currency. Exceptions will be made for bonds and securitised debts and for organised markets, where member states may take measures to convert the contracts into euro before the end of the transitional period, in order to synchronise the changeover of organised markets like stock exchanges.

The 'no compulsion, no prohibition' principle also applies to banks and to the public sector. In particular, using the euro in tax matters would require the consent of the tax authorities and special national legislation. During the transitional period, tax authorities are not obliged to accept the euro, either as a payment or in tax declarations. After the transitional period, all amounts expressed in national currencies will be converted into euro at the official conversion rates.

Legal tender

Legal tender means the form of payment which a creditor is legally obliged to accept in settlement of a debt (unless the parties have specifically agreed on some other form of payment). The legal tender concept is defined in national legislation. It covers notes and coins. The legal tender concept usually has little relevance in daily life: in general one knows which currency is accepted as a means of payment. In the changeover to the euro, however, this may change and people will become more aware of whether they are paying and accepting legal tender or not.

In the proposed legal framework, notes and coins denominated in a national currency will retain their legal tender status in their country of origin during the transitional period. Thus DM notes will be legal tender in Germany, but not in France or Portugal. As from 1 January 2002 at the latest, notes and coins denominated in euro shall be put into circulation. They will have legal tender status in all participating member states. This will not be affected by the small national symbols that may figure on the notes and coins. Thus a euro note with a small French symbol on it will be legal tender in Germany.

Notes and coins denominated in national currencies will retain their legal tender status until 30 June 2002 at the latest. This means that there will be a period of at most six months during which both the euro and the national currency have legal tender status. This period may be shortened by national law.

National currency notes and coins will not become valueless when they lose their legal tender status. The issuers — central banks and governments — will continue to exchange them against euros in accordance with the laws and practices of each member state for exchanging old notes and coins once new ones have been issued.

Continuity of contracts

Obviously, the changing of the denomination of a currency should not alter the terms of any contract. When, for instance, one owns a bond of DM 1000, having a coupon of 7.5% and maturing on 1 October 2005, the only thing that changes will be the replacement of the DM 1000 by the corresponding amount in euros at the fixed conversion rate. The bond will still have a coupon of 7.5% (but then related to the euro amount and paid in euros) and a maturity of 1 October 2005. All other conditions remain unchanged. The same goes for rental contracts, labour contracts, and so on. When the monetary law (*lex monetae*) of a state is changed, it does not affect the contract law (*lex obligationis*), which may even be third country law.

As explained in Chapter Nine, most legal experts see no reason to question the continuity of contracts. Nevertheless, in order to take away any possible doubt and to reduce the risks of needless litigation, Article 3 of the Commission's proposed Regulation B explicitly states that 'the introduction of the euro shall not have the effect of altering any term of a legal instrument or of discharging or excusing performance under any legal instrument, nor give a party the right unilaterally to alter or terminate a legal instrument. This provision is subject to anything which parties may have agreed'. The term 'legal instrument' means legislative provision, contract or unilateral legal acts.

Subdivisions and rounding
According to Article 109l.4 of the Treaty, the conversion rates can only be adopted on 1 January 1999. For the preparation of the changeover, in particular for the adaption of software, it is important to know as far in advance as possible how many significant figures the conversion rates will have and how converted amounts will have to be rounded. This will therefore be determined in the proposed Regulation B.

Conversion rates will be adopted with six significant figures. This follows the standard for the EMS. It means that a conversion rate, when counted from the left and starting by the first non-zero figure, has six figures. The DM/Euro rate would be something like 1.92692 and the LIT/euro rate 1935.41.[4] The six significant figures requirement does prevent it from ending in one or more zeros, even on purpose. For any conversion the official conversion rates will have to be used: conversion rates may not be rounded or truncated.[5]

As the conversion rates will be expressed in national currency per euro, all amounts expressed in national currencies will have to be divided by this rate in order to convert them into euros. So, using the (hypothetical) conversion rates mentioned above, DM 1000, 1 m and

1 bn would be converted to, euro 518.96, 518,962.90 and 518,962,904.53 respectively.[6]

Amounts converted into euro will have to be rounded to the nearest euro cent (Article 5). Monetary sums converted into national currencies will have to be rounded to the nearest sub-unit or unit of the national currency in accordance with national practices. When the conversion yields a result that is exactly half way, the sum shall be rounded up. Thus euro 1.055 (which would be a coincidence) would be rounded up to 1.06.[7]

The flexibility in the formulation of the rounding rules allows for the continuation of practices in some countries by which prices in particular are expressed in more decimals than the smallest sub-unit of the currency. This is for instance the case for petrol prices and for prices in long term contracts such as gas and electricity. For instance, electricity prices in Belgium are expressed in two decimals, whereas the smallest amount you can pay by bank transfer is one franc. Converting the current electricity price of BEF 2.23 per kwh (night tariff) would yield euro 0.0562, which gives more or less the same degree of precision as the BEF price. Rounding the price to the nearest euro cent would imply a price increase of 6.4%.

Only the conversion rates between the national currencies and the euro will be determined. No bilateral rates between national currencies will be given, because this could lead to inaccuracies in converting large amounts: going from one national currency to the other and then back again may not yield the original amount. For converting one national currency (NC) into the other one has to divide by the national currency NC1/euro rate and then multiply the amount by the NC2/euro rate, or, alternatively, multiply by the quotient of the two (provided it is expressed in a sufficient number of decimals, which may be much more than six). Whichever algorithm is used for this conversion, the result should always be the same as prescribed by Article 4(4) of the Commission's proposal, which provides for the intermediate euro amount to be rounded to at least three decimals.

Costs

An important issue is who will have to bear the costs of changing currencies from one denomination into the other. Two different cases have to be distinguished.

The first is the one-off changeover that will take place at the end of the transitional period, or sooner in cases where organised markets change over. When in a bilateral contractual relation the denomination of the contract changes, both parties are responsible for changing the denomination in their own accounts. The same applies of course to multilateral relationships. In particular, when bank accounts will have to be redenominated at the end of the transitional period, the banks will have to bear the costs of redenominating their accounting systems and the clients will have to bear the costs of the corresponding changes in their accounts.

Quite different is the case when during the transitional phase one wishes to change from one currency to the other. Suppose one has an account denominated in euro and wants to pay an amount denominated in one's own or a foreign national currency denomination. In those cases a bank may charge a fee for the administrative costs of having to change the denomination of the currency. Whether the bank really charges such a fee will depend on its strategy for the introduction of the euro and of course that of its competitors.

Sometimes the question is raised whether the costs for the changeover will be tax-deductible. In general, they will not be treated differently from normal expenditure for running a business, which reduce the taxable profits. This is, however, a matter of national legislation and one should turn to the national tax authorities for more detailed information.

Member state competence
Within the framework set by the proposed Council regulations, member states will have a certain degree of freedom to make specifications according to their own needs and desires.

In particular, the length of Phase C in which the euro as well as the national currency has the legal tender status, can be shortened by national law (Article 14 of Regulation A). Some member states are already considering a substantial shortening of this period, up to even a 'legal Big Bang' in which there is no dual legal tender situation. Also, the decision to redenominate outstanding debt during the transitional period and to allow organised markets to change the unit of account of their operating procedures can be taken at the member state level. However, other provisions imposing the use of the euro during the transitional period may only be adopted according to any time-frame laid down by Community legislation.

Other issues

The fact that all currencies of member state without a derogation will become a sub-division of the euro on 1 January 1999, makes it legally certain that there will be no exchange rate risk and that there will be no need for matching open positions in each currency. Consequently, for the purpose of prudential supervision, these currencies need to be considered as one currency. Provisions in national legislation prohibiting or limiting the use of other currencies of participating member states will automatically become obsolete.

All amounts in legal instruments will have to be converted at the end of the transitional period by using the official conversion rates. This also applies to amounts in national legislation, such as tax brackets, allowances, maximum fines to be imposed, and so on. Some of the amounts that were round figures in national currency will be an odd figure after conversion into the euro. If the national legislators want to 'clean up' these figures by introducing rounded euro amounts, this will have to be done by separate legislation.

The same goes for the nominal value of shares and bonds. For trading shares and bonds, the nominal value is not very important, it is the market value that matters. However, companies may want to clean up the value of nominal shares whenever they issue new shares. Technically this may be done by issuing additional stock such that each share is converted to a new one with a rounded value in euro.

---

[1] Commission Communication COM(96) 499, containing proposal 96/0249 (CNS), *Council Regulation on the Introduction of the Euro*, based on Article 235 and 96/0250 (CNS), *Council Regulation on Some Provisions Relating to the Introduction of the Euro*, based on Article 1091.4.

[2] By stating this, Regulation A is clearly classified as monetary law, which has general universal recognition.

[3] This figure is based on the 31 October 1996 ecu/BEF rate of 39.6941.

[4] These are the ecu rates as of 31 October 1996

[5] In some cases, for converting historical data of a 'foreign' participating currency, one may have to convert first to the home currency at the old exchange rate, and then to the euro at the official conversion rate.

[6] If the conversion rate had been expressed in euro/DM, conversion to the euro would be by multiplication. In the above example this would have yielded 518,965,18.963 and 518,963,000 respectively. It would however have led to a conversion rate like 0.000516686 for the LIT.

[7] This rule allows software programmes to add euro 0.005 and then ignore any digit after the second decimal of the result.

Chapter Nine

Continuity of Contract

Jacques Terray

On 1 January 1999, the euro will become the currency of the member states participating in monetary union. National currencies will become non-decimal expressions of the euro. What is the effect of these changes on the then outstanding money contracts? Most commercial or private transactions will not be affected to a significant extent. Sales of goods for example, or employment contracts, or apartment leases, will continue with the price, wages or rents still being paid in the same EMU currency unless the two parties agree to shift to euros.

On the other hand, the start of Stage Three may have an impact on those agreements in which a sum of money is not only the price for a good or a service, but is itself the object of the transaction. This category of financial contract is mainly composed of bank lending, debt instruments traded on a regulated market and derivative products.

One of the parties to a financial contract usually feels that it has not developed in a favourable manner. If that party can find a legal way out of the agreement, it may be tempted to use it.

The main issues which are likely to be raised in 1999 or later by dissatisfied parties belong to three main groups. The most obvious is the sudden and irrevocable change in the definition of the currency. Does this allow one party to claim that the agreement is impossible to carry out, and therefore has to be cancelled? Aside from the change in the currency, financial contracts often refer to market rates or indexes, such as the interbank money market rates, or the ecu basket of currencies. Those references will either disappear or be altered significantly in 1999. Will agreements continue? The last group of issues relates to derivative products, as they are designed to protect at least one of the parties against exchange rate or interest rate fluctuations. In 1999, conversion rates between EMU currencies will be irrevocably fixed and there will be money market rates only in euro. Some derivative contracts will thus become questionable. Should they be terminated?

It is crucial for the success of EMU that those legal issues be explored, then resolved as early as possible before 1999.

The available tools for such a resolution are (1) the monetary law, which will define for the entire world the value of the new currency, (2) each national body of law governing the law of contracts and place of payment, for example, and (3) recommendations of market associations both at national and international level.

Ultimately, if conflicts arise, it is for the courts to test these various tools and to assess the claims of the parties. For the last hundred years, through dramatic currency movements, the highest courts in the United States, England, France or Germany have built a rather consistent and unified body of precedents and guidelines.[1] Developing the European currency while ignoring that historical background would be like building without foundations.

Disappearance of national currencies

The highest courts in OECD countries, as well as The Hague Permanent International Court of Justice (in 1929) have confirmed the basic rule that each sovereign state has sole authority to define the currency of its country and to change that definition as it wishes. Sovereign states may also enter into treaties such as the Maastricht Treaty and grant to a treaty body, such as the European Central Bank, authority to decide the issue of a common currency.

The above *lex monetae* ensures that the decision of a foreign state, or a group of foreign states, to create a new currency or later on to change its definition should be recognised by the courts in a situation where such foreign currency is at stake, regardless of the law governing the contract, the nationality of the parties or the place of the transaction.

The proposed 'Council Regulation on Some Provisions Relating to the Introduction of the Euro' contains a brief provision (Article 3) on the continuity of contracts. This was contrary to the wishes of London-based market associations, who favoured much more detailed legislation on the continuity of contracts. The working group that prepared the draft regulation took the view that the introduction of the euro was not likely to affect existing contracts and that more detailed rules might have cast doubt on the generality of the solution.

The draft regulation also provides (Article 8) that EMU currencies are mere denominations of the euro. The effect on each party to a given contract of the choice between the euro and an EMU currency for a payment or for the calculation of an amount is thus minimised. As the euro and a given EMU currency are but different denominations of the same currency, it will be difficult for one party to bring evidence of damage it would suffer from the choice of one versus the other. Being thus based on a steady line of case law and on the rule that EMU currencies and the euro are one and the same, the draft regulation, when it is adopted, will adequately assure that contracts will not be rescinded, voided or otherwise affected simply because the euro has become the currency of the EMU.

Other contractual problems
It is a general view among practising lawyers and scholars, reinforced by the text of the Commission's proposed regulation, that a fixed interest rate in EMU currencies will not be affected by the introduction of the euro. In other words, 4.5% per annum denominated in an EMU currency will readily become 4.5% per annum in euro.

There is more room for uncertainty regarding the transactions or instruments associated with floating rates, at least until the European Monetary Institute delivers its report on the central money market, due before the end of 1996. Until then, it is not possible to predict whether domestic interbank market rates will be mirrored by the euro rates starting in January 1999. If not, then the new euro rate replacing the EMU currency may have some slight differences such as number of days per year, time of fixing, delivery terms, and so on.

In most countries, the courts have developed case law when an index, for example in food or rents, is no longer published. The general tendency is for judges to facilitate the choice of neighbour indices for the sake of continuity of the contract. The courts will find great support in their endeavours in any recommendation which may have been issued by the associations of the relevant trades such as treasurers, brokers or bankers. National central banks may also set guidelines for the transition of debt instruments from EMU currency rates of interest to euro rates.

Another concern of some of the market players is the likelihood of rate fluctuations of an unexpected magnitude. Their fear is linked with memories of the speculation which affected the French franc and the pound sterling in recent years during EMS crises. Would a court be tempted to interfere with the normal course of a transaction on the ground of contractual clauses which are standard in the financial markets and which are aimed at protecting the parties against disruptive legislation?

Most experts, such as the French working group report on legal issues raised by the single currency of 2 July 1996, have underlined the fact that monetary union, unlike most of the currency changes in the thirties has been prepared at least since the 1992 Maastricht Treaty in an orderly fashion, and is not the result of a monetary crisis. In those circumstances, it is hard to believe that either a court or an administrative authority would interfere with market forces and contractual provisions on the ground of rate fluctuations. Comments from common law countries on possible 'frustration' do not seem to convince even their authors.

Another area of relative uncertainty is the fate of ecu denominated debts after 1999. Either the contractual definition of the ecu merely refers to its official definition, which may be revised from time to time, and it becomes the euro when it is introduced. Or the contract explicitly provides for safeguards and escape clauses when calculation on the basket definition becomes impracticable (which is the case in many of the earlier credit agreements). The proposed regulation provides, in Article 2(1), that a reference to ecu in a contractual document which does not specify whether or not it is meant to be the official definition of the ecu, will be deemed to refer to the official definition. In other words, the party who challenges the one for one conversion rate between ecu and euro will have to prove that, when the agreement was signed or the instrument issued, the intention was not to adjust the definition of the ecu along the same rules as the official ecu. Such a challenge will in most cases be very difficult to prove. In any case, market associations will issue recommendations which will help the judges in their interpretation.

Derivative products

As underlined in the International Security Dealers Association (ISDA) response to the EC Green Paper (1 November 1995), the value of a derivative product is linked to the volatility of underlying exchange or interest rates. When that volatility disappears because the two currencies are linked to each other at an irrevocable conversion rate or when the two interest rates become based on the same central rate, what is the purpose of continuing the contract? This issue is to be solved in accordance with the law which governs the contract, and with the provisions of the contract. Master Agreements currently used in the market do not provide for a situation like the introduction of the euro. A change of currency is not a ground for termination of the transactions. The remedy of frustration does not seem available in England and there is no clearer indication in the United States, where court decisions have been rendered on totally different sets of facts. France has no remedy comparable with the frustration doctrine. However derivatives are *contrats aléatoires* (risky contracts) where unpredictability is an indispensable component at the time of entering into the contract. It seems, but there is a lack of relevant case law, that unpredictability need not continue for the whole duration of the contract.

Given the scarcity of case law and the lack of guidance from the law of contracts in most countries, it is important that market associations such as ISDA issue contractual provisions (such as their draft of 9 April 1996) in which parties agree that the introduction of the euro will not 'of itself' allow the termination of the contracts.

What are the recommendations that a practising lawyer would give to a treasurer in a group of companies or a bank at this stage of the EMU process? First, wait for:

- the Council decision (expected at the Dublin European Council in December 1996) on the proposed Council regulations on the legal framework;

- the EMI conclusions on the central money market (expected at the end of 1996);

- the final wording of the contractual provisions to be inserted in the ISDA Master Agreement, the IPMA (International Primary Market Association) rules and national associations (such as Association Française des Banques). It would seem unwise to use home made provisions which may conflict later with those adopted by the trade and render contracts less liquid.

Second, stimulate the associations so that they adopt simple, straightforward standard clauses whose main purpose will be to set a benchmark of good faith at the time of the introduction of the euro.

Third, check current financial contracts expiring after 1999 to ensure that none has provisions which are not in line with normal market practice in terms of currency exchange, interest calculation, termination clauses or illegality, and that no contract is based on options which might not be available after 1999.

---

[1]   For an authoritative survey of case law in England, France, Germany and the United States, see F.A. Mann, *The Legal Aspect of Money: with special reference to comparative private and public international law*, Oxford, Oxford University Press, 1992

Chapter Ten

Payment Systems

Claus F. Hilles

Payment systems form the core of monetary transactions. How easy will it be for banks to run a dual currency payment system?

For German banks, 16 August 1996 was an important milestone on the road to the euro. It was on this day that the 'Framework agreement on inter-company domestic payments for the introduction of the Euro currency' came into force between the associations of the German banking sector and the Bundesbank. This agreement forms the technical basis for handling national payments both in the transition phase, involving the duality of euros and DM, from 1999 to 2002 and for the final changeover to the euro in 2002.

The arrangements are very customer friendly in nature, since they give corporate customers in particular a sufficiently long run-up period of nearly 6 years for converting their electronic payments, and leave open the choice between DM and euros. For the German banking sector this agreement ensures the requisite planning certainty, while leaving a period of more than two years for making adjustments to complex computer systems. One particular advantage in this respect is the duty of complete digitisation from mid-1997 on, and the associated discontinuation of paper-based payments in business between German banks.

In particular, the agreement contains the following arrangements:

- starting on 1 January 1999, German banks will give the national data record format (data carrier exchange) in both the DM amount (as in the past) and the euro amount (new);

- settlements between German banks will be in euros only;

- accounts at Germany's state central banks and at the Deutsche Bundesbank will be kept exclusively in euro.

Apart from customers' wishes and each bank's changeover planning, this agreement ensures that, when the euro is launched, the structural basis will be in place for efficient payments and customer-friendly operations. The individual conversion of account-keeping to euros is likely to be influenced primarily by customers' operational considerations. In this respect, big multinational firms have a key role to play.

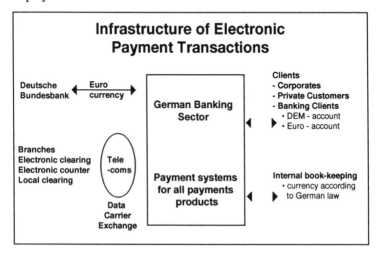

Infrastructure of Electronic Payment Transactions

One positive factor in this solution is the multifunctionality of the German data record format. It is used in all payment products (transfers, cheques, debit notes, credit card settlements, etc.) and is employed in all DM payment systems (EAF II, ELS, magnetic tape clearing, etc.).

The German payment system uses data records which consist of 21 fields (numbered C1 to C19), numeric as well as alpha-numeric. The record thus contains fields for the payer's name and account number, the receiver's name and account number, the amount to be transferred, the reason for payment, etc. The latter may have up to 351 characters or bytes. As it happens field C12, containing 11 digits, intended for codes to be used by large corporates, was rarely used, it was decided to use this field for transferring euro amounts. In Phase B the German payment record will therefore contain the amount to be transferred denominated in DM (field C9, 11 digits) as well as the amount denominated in euro (field C12, 11 digits). An unused reserve field in the payment record (C17, 3 digits) will be used to transfer information about the original order currency (DM or euro). Based on this, appropriate information can be forwarded to the recipient of the payment in the statement of account as follows:

Statement of Account no. 112	Dresdner Bank AG BLZ 500 800 00	
Account 1 926 252 00	Date 25.09.1999	Page 1
- Date — Value Date ───────────────────────────────		DEM ───
	Previous Balance Per	4.000,00 C
	19.09.1999	
20.09 20.09	Salary August 1999	3.588,26 C
	*** Euro 1.866,55 C ***	
22.09 22.09	Execution of your standing	1.200,00 D
	order/James Landlord/Rent	
	BLZ 50080000 ACC. 0123456700	
	New Balance	6.388,26 C
	INFORMATION/YOUR BALANCE IN EURO	3.323,06 C
MR MICHAEL SPECIMEN		

Bitte entsprechenden Vermerk auf der Rückseite beachten. / Please see reverse. / Se reporter au verso.

Accordingly, customers can still submit orders in DM, pending the final introduction of the euro in the year 2002. The supplement to the data record to include the euro amount and the original currency will be made by the major German banks or by the Bundesbank on behalf of smaller institutes. Shown in a diagram, the processing of a data record is illustrated in the table below.

In paper-based payments, customers in Germany will be confronted with the euro for the first time in the middle of 1997. As one of a few other changes, credit transfer orders, which are unitary in Germany, will already contain a currency field for completion by the remitter as in eurocheques.

Summing up, it can be said that for Germany, as far as domestic payments are concerned, the course is already set for a smooth transition and that those affected will have sufficient time to do the complex and cost intensive conversion work. In the competition between banking centres within a common currency, this is an important criterion.

General remarks

Whether other European countries will also be able to introduce a dual currency payment system, will amongst other factors depend on

Funds Transfer System/Issues Involved

Remitters Account Currency	Remitters Bank	German Payment Systems	Beneficiaries Bank	Beneficiaries Account Currency
DM	Conversion/ Completion Euro	Euro	Examination DM/Euro	DM
DM	Conversion/ Completion Euro	Euro	Examination DM/Euro	Euro
Euro	Conversion/ Completion DM	Euro	Examination Euro/DM	DM
Euro	Conversion/ Completion DM	Euro	Examination Euro/DM	Euro

the structure of their data records. Therefore having a dual currency payment system may be more complicated than in Germany and the total costs could be prohibitive.

When a dual currency payment solution is not feasible, one could consider changing the payment system into euros during Phase B, while the larger part of the economy is still denominated in national currencies. The euro denominated payment system would then have to process national currencies. Payment orders in national currencies would have to be converted to euros and back to the national currency after passing through the payment system. In those cases it should be ensured that the payment received is exactly the same as the original payment order. This may not always be the case if the smallest unit of the national currency is smaller than the euro cent. For instance, paying NLG 90 would yield (at the NLG/ecu rate of 6 November 1996) euro 41.61 after converting with a rate of 2.16281. Reconverting it to NLG yields 89.99 guilders. The difference of one cent would seriously complicate accounting. Therefore the payment system should be adapted to avoid these differences. A solution would be to have the euro amounts expressed in three decimals (in the example above, NLG 90 would be converted to euro

41.613 and then back to NLG 90.00); this would require an investment whose life, and therefore cost recovery, would be limited to Phase B. Such rounding problems do not arise when the smallest national currency unit is larger than the euro cent, as in Belgium.

Cross-border payments in EMU
Another issue is the making of cross-border payments within the EMU area. The establishment of EMU will make sure that the exchange rate costs of making a cross-border payment will disappear. This will slightly lower the total costs of making a payment. What remains is the cost of not having an integrated payment system at the European level. However, monetary union will facilitate the building of an integrated payment system in the long run. This is highly desirable so as to achieve a system where cross-border payments within Europe can be made at much lower costs than international payments today. This issue deserves more attention. Here, no definite common European approach is as yet evident that might ensure satisfactory cross-border customer service when it comes to dual currencies. The discussions at SWIFT (Society for Worldwide Interbank Financial Telecommunication) or ECBS (European Committee for Banking Standards) have generated no tangible results so far.

In particular, it is absolutely essential that the discussions already underway in the banking community on a new version of the ECBS standard EBS 200 make inroads in all national payment systems of each European country as a precondition for low cost operations. Equally helpful in promoting fully electronic processing would be an early implementation of the IBAN (International Bank Account Number) following the introduction of the euro.

THE CHANGEOVER AND COMBATING
MONEY LAUNDERING

Leo Verwoerd

The changeover from national currencies to euro notes and coins is a unique event that challenges our imagination. Instead of merely safeguarding the efficient implementation of the changeover, which is a sizeable task in itself, we may be tempted to add auxiliary objectives, such as the detection of dirty money.

1945

Older people in the Netherlands will almost certainly recall the spectacular money rehabilitation programme that took place, as in other European countries, shortly after the end of the second world war. On 26 September 1945 every person in the Netherlands received one new ten guilder banknote. All old notes instantly lost the status of legal tender, and all bank accounts were blocked. The main aim was to control the excessive money supply before hyperinflation could build up. Money supply had quadrupled during the war, mainly as a result of the influx of Reichsmarks which were converted into guilders. In addition, there had been huge government deficits during the war years: while national income dropped from five to three billion, government domestic debt rose from four to 22 billion guilders, of which 16 billion had a floating rate. Despite the quadrupling of money and the excessive government deficits, wages and prices had risen by only 50% in nominal terms during the entire war.

Although the main aim was to control the excessive money supply, the rehabilitation effort is remembered best for its other purpose, the confiscation of 'black money'. Several measures were taken. The amount of cash surrendered, and the identity of the owner, were recorded on so-called 'money cards'. Jewellers, antiquaries and the like were required to register all transactions and all advance payments for precious goods. All bonds and shares were registered and bank secrecy was abolished in order to enable the government to screen all bank accounts and all money cards, which represented cash. Individual bank accounts and money cards were only de-blocked if no black money was involved.

2002

The differences with the present day situation are huge: there is no need to decrease the money supply, a temporary blocking of all bank accounts is unthinkable, and so is a temporary withdrawal of virtually all cash. The main reason for such measures in 1945 was their monetary and economic unavoidability; in the modern economy of 2002 such measures could easily have serious negative monetary and economic consequences. Furthermore, in today's complex, interdependent and international economy, the very idea that the government could check, in a one off operation, the possible illicit character of the economic source of each and every banknote, without completely sealing the country for cross-border movements of cash, must be rejected.

Financial Action Task Force

Moreover, combating money laundering and safeguarding the integrity of the financial system have become much too important to wait for a one-off occasion. In 1990, the Financial Action Task Force (FATF), an independent task force of 26 major countries dedicated to combating money laundering, issued forty recommendations. Shortly thereafter, the European Union adopted a directive which obliges the member states to take statutory action against money laundering. Measures include prohibition and prosecution of laundering, identification of customers of financial institutions, disclosure of suspicious financial transactions, seizure and confiscation of the money, as well as international cooperation and asset sharing.

To date, all EU members have taken measures to detect money launderers during cash transactions with financial institutions. There are rules in place for identification of customers and the reporting of suspicious financial transactions to the authorities. There is no reason to make an exception for exchange transactions between national currency to the euro. First, customers making such exchange transactions will have to be identified just like in any other transaction, that is if the transaction exceeds the amount of ecu 15,000 mentioned in the money laundering directive (or any lower national threshold). Second, suspicious national currency to euro exchange transactions will have to be reported to the authorities, just like any other suspicious transaction. In the Netherlands, of all large currency exchange transactions presently reported, approximately one in seven is thought by the authorities to be linked to money laundering and is further investigated. The changeover from national currencies to euros is not in itself a legitimate reason to deposit large amounts of cash, or several smaller amounts in order to avoid the threshold for that matter. Such a deposit for which there is no other obvious reason than the customer having to visit the bank for the changeover anyway, must therefore be considered suspicious.

Naturally, because of the system in place, many cash guilders will show up outside the Netherlands in 2002. They will be offered to foreign banks, who will eventually ship them back to the country of origin. Today, over 30 major financial centre countries have anti-money laundering legislation in place. By the year 2002, their number will have increased considerably. We would expect financial institutions abroad to be obliged to report suspicious currency exchange transactions to the local authorities. International cooperation between judicial and police authorities should take it from there.

Chapter Eleven

Accounting Problems and Solutions

Leo van der Tas

The introduction of the euro will have major accounting implications for all companies. Even companies that have so far not made transactions in any foreign currency will be faced by the need to address the problem of currency translation in their accounts. This chapter will cover the accounting problems connected with the implementation of the euro in each of its three phases. It will not only deal with financial reporting issues, but also with management information systems. Possible solutions to those problems will be suggested.

Taxation issues are dealt with in Chapter Twelve. However, it will be necessary in this chapter to shed some light on the different systems applicable in the various member states regarding the link between tax return and financial report. This link may have a significant impact on the accounting treatment of the introduction of the euro.

Before we go into details, a description is needed of the measures that the EU has already taken in the accounting field. Foreign currency translation is a rather complex aspect of management and financial accounting. The EU Accounting Directives provide little guidance on financial reporting and contain no guidance on management accounting. The Fourth EEC Directive (Directive 78/660/EEC of 25 July 1978) on the annual accounting of certain types of company contains a requirement that companies must set out in the notes to the accounts which policy has been applied to translate foreign currencies, if applicable (Article 43(1)(i)). Directive 90/604/EEC of 8 November 1990 amended the Fourth Directive to include an Article 50a requiring member states to allow companies to publish their accounts in ecus by simply translating the accounts in local currency at the exchange rate against the ecu at balance sheet date. The exchange rate must be disclosed in the notes. However, it left to member states the right to require companies to draw up accounts in the national currency. In 1995 a document was published by the European Commission containing a working document of the Accounting Advisory Forum, a consultative body to the Commission consisting of representatives from organisations of preparers, users and auditors of accounts and accounting academics. This document (*Foreign Currency Translation*, Luxembourg, 1995) provides guidance on the translation of foreign currencies in financial reports. In this chapter, this document will be referred to where appropriate.

The special characteristic of the euro is that it is not only a translation but more of a replacement of currencies which creates problems not covered by any of the above-mentioned documents, nor any other accounting standard.

When to change over

The question arises of when, during the transitional period between 1999 and 2002 companies should change their reporting currency into euros. This question will depend on the circumstances of the company. In some member states companies are allowed to draw up and publish their accounts in a currency other than the local currency. All member states already allow companies to publish their accounts in ecus. In those countries where companies are allowed to draw up and publish their accounts in another currency, some have decided to choose the US dollar or Japanese yen as the reporting currency because virtually all of their activities are taking place in dollars or yen. In that case the introduction of the euro will probably have hardly any effect on the company because it is just one other foreign currency. The impact is no different from that on the accounts of a US or Japanese company reporting in its own currency. This example is, however, an exception. All other companies will be influenced in one way or another and will have to decide when to change over to the euro.

During Phase A it will not be possible to report in euros, simply because the euro does not exist. It will, however, be possible to switch to reporting in ecus, as a transitional measure. It will also be possible, as many companies are already doing at this moment, to provide additional information in ecus, alongside the information in national currencies.

During Phase B it will be allowed and possible to publish accounts in euros. It can be presumed that member states will also be required to allow companies to draw up their accounts in euros because the ecu will have been changed into the euro and because member states are already required to allow companies to have their accounts published in ecus. From the financial year 2002 onwards companies will no longer be allowed to report in the national currency because this currency will no longer exist.

The exact timing of the transition to the euro in Phase B or C will differ from company to company. It may also be variable within one company for different purposes. For example, if the national tax authorities only allow the company to file their tax returns in euros by the end of the transitional period, the company may choose to use euros beforehand for internal management information and financial reporting purposes. Preferably, the changeover will coincide with the launch of new accounting software in the company, to take account of the euro. But this will not be necessary for financial reporting or income tax return purposes. It will be possible to take the output of the old accounting software in the national currency and translate the outcome at the exchange rate at balance sheet date. The change to the euro for management information purposes can hardly be done before the electronic data processing systems have been adapted to the new currency because it has an effect on the reporting systems in all layers of the organisation and requires all detailed information to be available in euros. The introduction of the new software is the subject of Chapter Thirteen.

First financial report in euros: which rate of exchange

During the first financial period in which the euro is the reporting currency, the financial position at the start of the period will have to be converted into euros from the national currency at the end of the preceding financial period. There are two ways of performing this conversion:

A. All balance sheet items in national currency on the balance sheet of the preceding period are translated at the fixed exchange rate against the euro. This is the easiest method.

B. The balance sheet in euros is prepared as though the company has always prepared its financial report in euros. This would mean that past transactions in local currencies would have to be treated as transactions in a foreign currency (from the perspective of the euro) and translated at the historical exchange rate between the national currency and the euro. Although from a technical point of view this would be the best method, it is very costly and time-consuming and it would also be very difficult to perform because of a lack of historical exchange rates. The exchange rate against the ecu is a bad surrogate because of the difference in character between the euro and the ecu.

Given the fact that it is virtually impossible to apply method B it is very unlikely that this method will be required in any member state. Depending on the accounting principles applied, method A might lead to some odd situations, particularly if a company has entered into transactions in other EMU currencies. Consider the following example (all exchange rates are fictitious and chosen for purposes of illustration only):

In 1996 the German company ABC, reporting in DM borrows FFr 1 m. At that time the exchange rate of the FFr against the DM is 4:1. The German company will report a long term loan of DM 250,000 on the liability side of its balance sheet. At the end of 1998 the exchange rate of the FFr against the DM has changed to 5:1. This implies a potential profit for the German company because the FFr 1 million which they will have to pay back is now worth only DM 200,000. According to German accounting principles, for prudential reasons, this potential profit is not yet shown in the accounts until it is realised (upon actual payment). However, for prudential reasons, potential losses would be shown as a loss. The reason for not showing the profit at this point but taking any losses into account lies in the fact that the exchange rate might fall back to 4:1 in which case at a later stage a loss would have to be reported. Let us presume that both Germany and France join EMU from the start and the exchange rate of the euro against the FFr and DM is set as follows: FFr 10 = DM 2 = euro 1. In this case the loan in FFr is converted into a loan in euros. The amount is now euro 100,000 which will have to be paid by the German company. So one would expect the German company to report a loan on its balance sheet of euro 100,000. Method A, however, leads to the German company showing a loan of euro 125,000 (the amount at which the loan is presented on the balance sheet in DM on 31 December 1998 is DM 250,000, the exchange rate against the euro is 1:2 so the amount in euros on 1 January 1999 is 125,000).

In the Netherlands and the United Kingdom another set of accounting principles is applied to account for foreign currency transactions. According to these principles, changes in the exchange rate against foreign currencies are accounted for, and shown as a profit or loss irrespective of the fact that the profit or loss may not yet have been realised in the form of cash. The reason for this policy is that this shows the real worth of the monetary assets and liabilities. If at a later stage the exchange rate were to change back, this would be an event where the loss should be attributed to the later financial period. Applying this principle to the above-mentioned example would mean that the German company ABC would show the French loan on its balance sheet in DM at an amount of DM 200,000 instead of DM 250,000. The difference would be shown as a profit in the financial year in which the exchange rate change occurred. Method A would in that case lead to an amount in euros of 100,000 which is the real amount to be paid by the German company.

The examples shown above are meant to illustrate the fact that applying method A to the first financial report in euros may have different effects in different member states and might lead to confusion in some countries. One way to bypass this problem is to consider the fixing of the exchange rates between EMU currencies as a realisation of currency exchange differences.

Does fixing mean realising?

A question raised by the changeover to the euro is whether the fact that the exchange rates between EMU currencies are irrevocably fixed implies a realisation of as yet unrealised exchange rate differences and would have to be shown as a profit or loss. This question is of course only relevant in those cases where unrealised exchange rate differences are deferred or not accounted for (such as under German accounting principles in the case of an unrealised profit, as illustrated in the example above). This is standard practice in many member states in the case of unrealised exchange rate gains. No member state allows the deferral of unrealised exchange rate losses. Several points of view can be taken:

- The gain has not been realised because no cash-flows have yet taken place so no profit is shown.

- It has been realised but should not be shown as a profit but instead should be deferred until the actual cash-flow has taken place (the loan is settled).

- It has been realised but should not be shown as a profit and should instead be taken directly to net equity.

- It has been realised and should be shown as a profit.

From an economic point of view the fourth position would be the most adequate because no exchange rate risks remain. However, this position may lead to adverse tax effects because if the unrealised gain were also taxed a company would be forced to pay taxes before it actually received the money connected to this gain. This might cause serious liquidity and solvency problems. Therefore, for tax purposes the second might be a practical compromise solution. The same arguments hold for financial reporting if local law requires the company to pay out a minimum percentage of its profit. In that case the company may be forced to pay a dividend although no money is available.

In the light of these tax consequences it is important to have some background information on the relationship between the tax return and financial report. In some member states such as the Netherlands and the UK, the two are considered as separate reports in which different accounting methods may be applied. In the majority of the member states, however, the link between the two is rather tight. The financial report is the starting point for the tax return so in order to benefit from tax advantages it is necessary to take account of them in the financial report. This means that in some countries companies would be able to apply the fourth method in the financial report and the first or second in the tax return. In the majority of countries this is not possible, inclining companies to apply the method which is the most advantageous from a tax point of view (the first or second).

Given the tax consequences of the various methods of accounting for the introduction of the euro it is important that national tax authorities make the introduction income tax neutral. This would be the case if taxation were to take place in the same financial period irrespective of the introduction of the euro. So even if in the financial report the exchange gain is recognised in the profit and loss account it should be possible for tax purposes to defer the gain until cash realisation has taken place (the first or second method).

It has to be taken into consideration that not all exchange rate gains and losses are shown as a profit or loss, even if they are realised. Some of them are accounted for directly in the net equity of the company, without passing through the profit and loss account. The Accounting Advisory Forum document on foreign currency translation mentions some examples:

- Exchange rate gains and losses on the investment in a foreign entity (subsidiary or affiliated company)

- Exchange rate gains and losses on loans provided to those foreign entities or loans received from them;

- Exchange rate gains and losses on loans entered into to finance the investments in foreign entities and denominated in the same currency.

The reasons for the different treatment are rather technical and details can be found in the document itself. Importantly, not all exchange gains and losses from the introduction of the euro are shown in the profit and loss account. Some go directly to net equity anyway.

Safeguarding the comparability of historical data

When changing over to the euro the risk arises, both in financial and management accounting, of losing comparable historical data. This will be the case if historical data in foreign EMU currencies is converted directly into euro amounts at the fixed exchange rate instead of first being converted into national currency amounts at historical rates. Consider the following example:

> The French subsidiary of a German company reports its financial results in FFr to its parent. The net turnover of the French subsidiary was exactly the same (FFr 100 m) in 1997, 1998 and 1999. The exchange rate of the DM against the FFr was 4:1 in 1997, 4.5:1 in 1998 and 5:1 in 1999. These rates are purely fictitious and only for illustration purposes. So the

German company, in its own accounts, exchanges this information into DM at the prevailing exchange rates. It considers the subsidiary to have a declining net turnover of DM 25 m in 1997 to DM 20 m in 1999. The perception of the performance of the French subsidiary from the point of view of the German company is different from the perception of the local management of the subsidiary. Multinational companies have learned to live with this exchange rate problem. The problem with the introduction of the euro is that it will enhance confusion. Let us have a look at the amounts in euros of the subsidiary after introduction of the euro in 1999 at an exchange rate of FFr 10 = DM 2 = euro 1. The German parent will convert the historical amounts in DM into euro at the fixed rate of 2:1. The French subsidiary will convert its historical net turnover amounts in FFr into euros at the fixed rate of 10:1. The result is the following:

	1997	1998	1999
Net turnover in euros according to French subsidiary	10.0 m	10.0 m	10.0 m
Net turnover in euros according to German parent	12.5 m	11.1 m	10.0 m

The same amounts in the same currency differ, creating some confusion between the French subsidiary and the German parent. However, this is nothing new. They are used to living with different amounts of the same item in different currencies. Now the same occurs in the same currency. It may be reassuring that this only occurs temporarily during the first years after the introduction. From 1999 onwards there will be no difference between the amounts in euros as calculated by the German parent and the French subsidiary. So the problems attached to historical data decrease with the number of years passing after 1999.

Balance of advantage

The problems of rounding and transfer of payments are discussed elsewhere in this book. Here we focus attention on a practical accounting problem which may arise if during the transitional periods rounding leads to payments received deviating slightly from payment orders. If, for example, an invoice of NLG 100 is paid by giving a bank the order to make a payment to the bank of the party the invoice originated from, and the transfer of money between banks takes place in euros, the payment received by the beneficiary may be NLG 99.99. Although the difference is only one cent, the aggregate of all rounding differences may not be an insignificant amount. Moreover, those tiny differences cause an amount of extra work. Normally, the financial EDP systems match payments received automatically with amounts outstanding (debtors). If differences are encountered, no matter how small, exception reports are produced which have to checked. The list of exceptions may become very long unless this problem of rounding is solved by the banks. So this is another reason for banks to deal very carefully with the rounding problem in payment transfers.

Concluding remarks

From an accounting point of view there are numerous advantages attached to the introduction of the euro. First, cost savings occur on currency translation for companies with operations in different EMU countries. Second, there will be less confusion between parents and subsidiaries because of currency exchange rate differences. Third, the common currency will make financial reports and management reports more transparent for the foreign reader, as they will not be distracted from the essentials simply because of a lack of feeling for the value of a another national currency.

On the other hand, the introduction of the euro will cause large initial costs in terms of adaptation of software, documents and reports. These, however, are temporary so the long run effect can be considered positive.

Chapter Twelve

The Changeover and Taxation

John Chown

The transition to the single currency should give rise directly to no tax problems. Accounts will be translated from domestic currency into euros, all relevant tax attributes should be carried over and VAT input and output calculations would continue (translated) as before. That said, tax law relating to foreign exchange has become incredibly complex and on the precedents it would be astonishing if something somewhere did not go wrong and that whatever it is will not be something anyone foresaw. We begin, therefore, by spelling out a few general principles outlining danger areas, and go on to show how these might possibly affect the transition.[1]

Although most of this chapter assumes we are dealing with a country which actually adopts the euro, the final section considers what would happen if monetary union goes ahead but a particular country, such as the United Kingdom, either opts to remain outside or fails to meet the Maastricht criteria. In this event, we suggest some tax measures that could be taken by government, specifically in this case the UK government, which would both encourage international business to continue to conduct its activities and leave the door open for a future change of mind.

Taxation problems with foreign exchange

The tax treatment of foreign exchange and of financial derivatives has notoriously been riddled with traps — and opportunities. For years there was little explicit law, and the more glaring anomalies arose from what the law did not say. The main English speaking countries have introduced new legislation (in the UK effective only from 23 March 1995) designed to make the taxation of foreign exchange and of derivatives more rational, which ought to mean the company treasurer could manage foreign exchange and interest rate exposure without a tax specialist at his side. Did it succeed? The short answer is no, if only because of the horrendous length and complexity of the relevant legislation. The UK has jumped from too little to too much law. In most other member states the law tends to be silent on these specific issues, although they have been spared the worst horrors of the past.

In the UK during the first period, the running was made by a small group of tax economists, plus the in-house tax specialists of some multinationals. Often the hardest part of their job was to convince the company's auditors and lawyers (there were outstanding exceptions) that there was in fact a problem. Now that the lawyers and accountants have some actual law they can get their teeth into, they have discovered the subject and can advise in detail on the complex statutory provisions. But there is a danger that some of these may still not understand the overall picture, and the intelligent treasurer, finance director or banker needs to keep a close eye on at least the more general aspects of the subject. Ignorance can be very expensive, and as recent cases show, not only because of tax problems. This is particularly true when the organisation also employs 'quants' or 'rocket scientists' using advanced techniques: will they and the international tax specialists be able to understand each other, and reconcile their different concepts?

The more serious problems arise mostly in the English-speaking countries and of course they can affect American, Canadian, or Australian companies with European Union subsidiaries. Most Continental European countries in principle tax companies on a comparison of net worth or accounting basis which avoids the complexities of the capital/revenue divide. They tend to have, and arguably to need, very little explicit legislation on the taxation of foreign exchange and derivatives. However, anomalies, particularly on timing, and the opportunity for the creative use of derivatives may be starting to create in a more modest way the same type of problem that has beset the UK and the US. Changes in law can be expected as these markets develop, and this could throw up problems affecting annual interest and annual payments which are not interest. The attempt to apply these categories to modern financial techniques has produced perverse results unacceptable to both taxpayers and tax collectors.

Tax analysis
The United States' discussion and legislation explicitly and helpfully distinguishes between three key factors in analysing the tax problem.

- First, what is the character of the transaction for tax purposes? Is it a capital gain (or loss), a regular income item or a 'nothing'? Nothings have in the past included capital liabilities, assets which constitute debts 'not on a security', government securities and qualifying corporate bonds, and (more recently) their derivatives. This has been a central issue in the UK giving rise to tax fragmentation. It is also important in the United States and other English-speaking countries, but less so in Continental Europe.

- Second, what is the timing of the transaction? Do we have to bring transactions into the tax computation only on a realisations basis, or do we bring into account unrealised profits and losses on a mark to market basis? A third possibility is amortisation, the writing of a cost or benefit over the life of a long term contract. This has now become a major issue in the UK although for many years it was swamped by the character question. It is probably now the key issue in Continental Europe.

- Third, what is the source of the gain or loss, domestic or foreign? This is an issue which mainly concerns the United States with its complex rules for taxing foreign-source income. Again a US parent will have to watch these points. There are particular traps in controlled foreign corporation type-legislation where the profits (but not necessarily the losses) of a subsidiary can be deemed to be those of the parent. This is another case of the symmetry problem.

Specific problems affecting the changeover

At the start of Phase B the currencies will be irrevocably fixed and the euro will be used in parallel with the domestic currency. Transferring between the euro and various domestic currencies will constitute a foreign exchange transaction but there should be no effective gain or loss, apart from a possible timing point. In Phase C, domestic currency would have to be converted into euros, at a rate of exchange which would have been known for some time.

Apart from the general tax uncertainties on fluctuations, there is one potential problem which may need to be examined in all relevant countries. Suppose a company has long term assets (or liabilities) in a foreign currency, and the gains or losses are not required to be marked to market under the relevant tax law. If there is a substantial unrealised profit in DM, will the conversion of this into euros be deemed to be a transaction precipitating an immediate tax liability? Conversely, if there is a non-realised loss, for example, on a DM bond liability, will its conversion into euros turn it into a domestic currency transaction treated for tax purposes as a nothing? It is probable but not certain that this is taken care of in present UK legislation and one may hope that all states would take measures to clarify the position before changeover.

What if the UK does not join?

This section mainly concerns the UK but could have application elsewhere. Whether or not the UK joins EMU, the country has every intention of remaining the natural base for non-Europeans expanding into Europe, having certain natural advantages, including language. The countries in Europe, including the UK, which use the 'imputation' system of corporation tax have a specific problem — surplus Advance Corporation Tax or equalisation tax — which several of them, again including the UK, have taken not altogether adequate steps to correct. These problems, preventing true Europe-wide holding companies, will seem even more anomalous after the introduction of a single currency.

Another factor discouraging the use of UK holding companies is that they are within the charge to capital gains tax on the disposal of subsidiaries. Apart from disposals in the normal course of managing a group, this could amount to an exit tax if it were ever decided, for whatever reason, to remove the top company of the group from the UK. Such gains are calculated in sterling and although indexation gives some protection at present, there could be a fear that if the UK were not a member of EMU, a sharp depreciation could be expensive for those international groups based in the UK. Capital Gains Tax is a mess of a tax, combining punitively high rates with a large and growing range of exceptions relieving many from the charge, and is in serious need of reform.

One change which would be of great help in these circumstances would be to permit UK companies that are part of international groups to make up their accounts in euros as a local currency (what the Americans, preferably, call 'functional currency'), and for those accounts to be accepted for tax purposes. The legal provisions already exist, and a clear announcement that this would be encouraged would send a positive signal to both investors and our EU partners. An incidental advantage is that if the UK inflation rate were significantly higher than the euro inflation rate, companies accounting in the euro would not suffer the (usually small) additional tax burden resulting from taking into account non real profits. This would give the government an incentive to avoid inflation which can only be to the benefit of all. Such a proposal was made in 1989, but the tax aspects were omitted in later versions as inflation rates had by then converged.[2]

[1]   John Chown, *Tax Efficient Foreign Exchange Management*, London, Woodhead Faulkner, 1990.

[2]   John Chown and Geoffrey Wood, *The Right Road to Monetary Union*, in Russell Lewis (ed.), *Recent Controversies in Political Economy*, London, Routledge, 1992.

Chapter Thirteen

Software

Ian P. Lynch and Alec Nacamuli

Today, only the smallest company can contemplate running its business without the aid of information technology (IT) in almost every corner of the operation: production and quality assurance, personnel systems and of course book-keeping. It is ironic that decimalisation in the Britain of the early 1970s was probably made easier by the widespread reliance on manual systems.

Since businesses are expected to be among the chief beneficiaries of the single currency, it is important they understand the scale of the challenge and adopt a systematic approach. Moreover, it must be recognised that investment will have to start before all the facts about the single currency's introduction are known, including which countries will be participating. This guide is designed to help companies 'EMU-proof' their systems while optimising the pace and scale of investment.

Issues

Can the implementation of the euro be reduced to a straightforward technical matter, in a similar manner to managing the well-known computer problems associated with the year 2000? While there are some similarities to the approach which needs to be adopted, the euro is considerably more complex and challenging for a number of reasons:

- the scope of all the systems which process 'value' in a business;

- the different treatments and uses of value in those systems;

- the mixture of mandatory and optional changes;

- the effects of timing on the different solutions adopted;

- the intricacies of managing the euro along the whole value chain.

The transition to the single currency should not however be viewed solely as an accounting and IT issue. It should provide the opportunity for the company to fundamentally re-examine its business strategy taking into account the opportunities and threats of monetary union: Is there a demand for new products and services in its line of business? Can existing product lines be exported? Are foreign competitors likely to penetrate existing markets? Do costs need to be reduced to remain competitive? How can operations and processes be rationalised?

To ensure that these issues are addressed, we recommend that companies establish a structure, as follows:

- a Mr/Ms Euro should be appointed as project leader;

- working groups should be established to examine the impact of the euro on all business lines and activities. These groups should include business and marketing, as well as IT and finance staff;

- regular review meetings should be held with the top management of the company;

- staff training and communication to customers should be addressed early on.

Following approval of the structure, a detailed project plan should be drawn up and communicated as widely as possible. This will have to incorporate every system in the business that counts, accounts for, disburses or in any way manages anything with a monetary value, such as accounts payable, accounts receivable, cash management, fixed asset register, general ledger, labelling, packaging, payments, payroll, pensions, production, risk management, sales and marketing, share registry and stock control.

A company's suppliers and customers will have their own systems and these also have the potential to cause problems and raise costs if they are not properly positioned for the euro. For example, if a customer's purchasing introduces rounding errors into its calculations, they may remit an incorrect amount in settlement of an invoice, causing expensive reconciliation and even credit management problems. Considering the number of suppliers and customers a company has to deal with, it is certain that problems like this will be a common feature at the outset of the single currency, and a well-run business will plan exception processing accordingly.

The phased introduction of the euro produces a period of three to four years when the national currency will be used alongside the single currency. It is true that the euro will be most visible in the financial markets, but even here there is no true dividing line. An investment bank may decide to make an early switch to the euro for internal systems because most of its business involves instruments denominated in euro rather than the national currency, but paying its employees is a retail transaction and payroll systems may not be converted at the same time.

It is important to remember that the principle of 'no prohibition, no compulsion' will be operating during the period 1999-2002, so there is unlikely to be a common timetable for making the switch for all categories of customer or supplier. This may require the company to be able to handle both denominations for up to four years. Whatever the eventual approach to the dual pricing problem, the underlying issue is the circulation of two versions of what is actually the same currency. Companies have four basic options for coping with this dual denomination period. The arguments for and against each approach are as follows:

1. The most comprehensive solution is to move to a completely multi-currency accounting system, where all transactions must have an explicit record of their currency, which could be one of several commonly traded or used by the company.

2. Options two and three are very similar, in that the internal book-keeping remains currency-blind, that is, all transactions and balances share one common, but implicit currency. Whether operated by the company or by a third party such as a bank, the function of a converter is to shield the core accounting from the dual denomination problem by applying a currency test to each transaction as it passes through the system.

3. The final option is to treat euro-denominated transactions exactly like foreign currency ones today — as exceptions — with special handling and accounting arrangements. After a 'Big Bang' conversion at the company level (presumably in 2001-02), it would be national currency transactions that would be treated as foreign.

The decision for and against each of these options is crucially dependent on the specific nature of the company: its lines of business, its suppliers and customers, the quality and profile of its existing systems, and so on. In the majority of cases, some combination of these options is going to be needed, and success will come from achieving the right balance.

THE DUAL DENOMINATION PERIOD (1999-2002)

OPTION	FOR	AGAINST
1. Make every system fully multi-currency	Future-proof and offers greatest functionality. Most flexible for any EMU scenario. Present value for exporters, etc.	Unnecessary for most systems which deal predominantly in one currency only. ''Rolls-Royce' response to a temporary problem.
2. Build or install converters to insulate systems	Can be decommissioned after 2002. Avoids changing the applications themselves. Allows for trading partners to convert to the euro on their own timetables. Makes sure the conversion is done right, by re-using the same logic.	Extra overhead on currency-blind systems which have previously been able to treat all transactions alike. Source currency of transactions may not be clear. Testing will be expensive as converters are introduced, reversed and finally removed.
3. Use conversion services from banks, etc.	Could be lowest-cost solution. Share in economies of scale & quality, as costs of development, testing and operation are spread over many customers. Easiest to switch off in 2002.	May not address intra-company transactions excuse for not tackling necessary issues in-house. Same drawbacks as converters in Option 2.
4. Handle on exception basis until internal 'Big Bang' in 2002	Lowest up-front cost. Uses relatively cheap resources, i.e. clerks. Benefits if EMU delayed, cancelled or reversed, i.e. no wasted investment in changing systems or installing converters. Opportunity to switch to the euro from an improved systems platform.	Higher operating costs if labour is more expensive than technology. Gamble on minimal 'seepage' in 1999-2002. High project risk of 'Big Bang'. Supplier/customer actions make it unmanageable.

The role of accounting packages

Can a business avoid most of the problems of operating during the transition period by relying on software suppliers to release EMU-proof versions of their packages, depending on which option it chooses for coping with the euro? The vendors themselves are generally confident. Indeed, multi-currency modules or versions of many of the most popular packages already exist. Their take-up has been relatively modest in terms of preparation for the euro because, it is believed, there is insufficient understanding of the day-to-day implications of the dual denomination period of 1999-2002.

Users of such packages should make sure that their planning does not underestimate the difficulty of moving from a currency-blind approach to a multi-currency system, while maintaining continuity in terms of operations and financial control. Early consideration should be given, in discussion with external auditors, of changes that may be required in the statement of accounts because of the euro. Additional running costs need to be allowed for, at least during the transition, and an estimate made of the hardware and software platform that will be needed to deliver the required performance. In some companies, there may be the intention to move from a centralised system to a more distributed client-server approach: such plans must be reviewed for compatibility with the accounting approach needed for the euro.

Of course, a relatively smooth upgrade path assumes two things: the supplier of the software is still in business, and the package itself is still being supported and upgraded. If this is not the case, then the customer could be in a worse situation than with an in-house developed bespoke system, since the underlying code may be commercially or technically inaccessible. There may be no alternative to replacement.

Opportunities

While it may seem difficult enough simply to cope with the shift to the euro, it would be a huge missed opportunity if all that effort and expense were to leave the business with the same frustrations and limitations as before. Companies with operations in several countries should look at where certain activities are carried out, and whether there is scope for centralisation or re-engineering. Treasury activities, for example, will be affected very early into EMU as the single capital market for the euro begins to take shape. There should certainly be scope for more efficient use of working capital once the exchange rate barrier is no longer there.

If the working capital itself is to be controlled more efficiently, that will require all the supporting systems to be enhanced to cope with the new environment. Not only cash management, but stock control and accounts receivable operations will be affected by the single currency, offering opportunities to standardise around fewer software packages, perhaps, or to reduce the number of sites carrying out the same functions.

One of the driving forces behind the single currency is to help in the operation of the single market in Europe, and so any transition planning needs to challenge the product and business managers on how they plan to exploit the new financial environment. The systems and operations implications of those strategies also need to be folded into the plan, and this will be most successful when the IT and operations areas are able to articulate some of the new options the business faces.

Solutions

There may be tools to speed up some of the analysis and conversion work, but there are no short cuts to understanding exactly what the transition scenario needs to be in a company. Certainly, it is helpful to start from an orderly applications and information architecture that is well documented and based on standard software platforms and languages. Unfortunately, few companies will be that well-placed and so the approach needs to start with the basics.

1. Bringing software inventory up to date

Perhaps this has already been done as part of the response to 2000. In any case, all the systems and their supporting programs need to be tagged and grouped for subsequent analysis. This is a good time to log how each system treats currency, from currency-blind to fully multi-currency. Of course, since it will be the business of the future that needs to cope with the euro, firms should try and take account of planned and likely upgrades, replacements and developments.

It is not too early for a business to open dialogue with its application software vendors, since the availability of a euro-enabled version of its accounting software, for example in late 1998, will have a ripple effect throughout its conversion plan. By the same token, the client demand for such an upgrade will obviously influence when they might bring it to market.

2. Explaining the business transition scenario for 1997-2003

At a high level, everyone needs to understand the stance of a company through different phases of the single currency's introduction. When will different business lines start using the euro? How will that correspond to moves by suppliers and customers? What pace of change is expected at different times. For example, will retailers find most of the change is bunched around late 2001, early 2002? What are the earliest or latest times it will be possible to make these changes? This company-specific business transition scenario is vital to the next stage of the planning.

3. Gap analysis

The scenario should suggest, in broad terms, when the major systems will need to switch over to the euro. When the changeover is complete, what currency-handling features will be appropriate for each system? Some will be able to return to being currency-blind. Gap analysis will further detail the nature of the change required system by system. Assuming scarce or at least finite systems and management resources, the order and priority of activity will start to emerge at this point.

4. Planning the transition

Once a business has defined the requirements at each stage of the transition to the single currency in terms of what systems are affected, this is the time to choose between the various options discussed above. Once again, a dialogue with software vendors is essential, since the changeover generates multiple buy-or-build decisions. Some systems will be too old, fragile or non-standard to warrant the re-investment of switching to the euro, so alternatives must be quickly examined and scheduled.

The type of decision-making process in an organisation is important; in particular, the time taken to choose between accounting packages last time, and the question of whether it will have the management time to do things the same way. Dealing with this problem is clearly bound up with the culture of a business, but it is likely that very hierarchical companies, for example, will need to streamline their procedures and committees. Management of the overall project will be extremely demanding for most companies, and can only succeed where actions and decisions are delegated to the right level.

5. Allowing for testing

The proportion of development time that is needed for testing is always surprisingly high to non-technical managers. This will be especially true of EMU, since there is no comparable event to act as a comparison. Even with the most rigorous testing, it is also unavoidable that bugs and other problems will emerge in new and altered systems, so companies should expect their software maintenance activity to be proportionately higher in the years following EMU. One would hope that proper testing will have identified the most glaring errors, like conversion rates being the wrong way round. Organisations should also ensure that they have sufficient capacity to carry out the testing, either in-house or otherwise, remembering that a large number of businesses will be reaching the testing stage at the same time.

It is a truism in the software industry that although individual components and sub-programs may work fine in isolation, there can still be unexpected problems when they are assembled together into systems. That is why careful coordination is necessary between the technical teams responsible for the detailed changes.

There will probably be limited time for multi-enterprise testing, but where there is a particularly close systems linkage with a key customer or supplier, it is worth allocating time to make sure that the euro-enabled systems will mesh together satisfactorily after the change.

6. Making the change

One peculiar element of the changeover is that the conversion rates themselves, the irrevocable rate at which the participating currencies are locked into EMU, are not likely to be known until immediately before 1 January 1999. Systems which need to be ready at the outset of EMU must have the capability of the rates being dropped in at short notice.

Some limited use of the basket ecu may be useful for ironing out some of the final kinks in the systems and giving people some familiarity with what the transition scenario will entail (while remembering that the basket ecu, of course, is not fixed against any of the national currencies).

A project of this scope and duration will also face problems of stamina, staff turnover and motivation. No matter how effective the project chief, there is no avoiding the need to have all the elements of the plan adequately documented, with appropriate skills transfer taking place between staff, vendors and consultants.

7. Decommissioning transitional solutions

This may seem obvious, but the project does not end on 1 July 2002, when the euro has fully replaced the national currencies (according to the plan). There will be a number of systems, software converters, third party services, and so on that need to be turned off in order for the business to reach its optimal configuration for the single currency.

This chapter has tried to give a roadmap of how to create a transition plan that dovetails the needs of the business with the external timetable for EMU and the single currency. We have emphasised the need for a common view of the priorities and major milestones within that plan and a streamlined approach to getting the job done, both internally and in partnership with vendors and other service providers.

Such a plan probably needs to be in place early in 1997 to be ready for EMU on time. It will need high level management support to ensure the plan is not blown off course over its six-year life, but that does not mean that there should not be changes and improvements along the way. Market requirements shift, new technology and software tools increase the options for achieving business goals, governments and central banks change their minds, and the best project management will be able to incorporate such factors into the plan as it evolves and moves into implementation.

The promise of the single currency is that eventual benefits outweigh the costs of conversion. Since at least 40% of those costs will be incurred in changes to IT systems, this will be the crucial battleground for the whole exercise, and the winners will be the companies who plan and execute a coherent transition to the euro. Failure will leave a company weakened and distracted for years — which is a dangerous condition in an ever more competitive environment in Europe and beyond.

Chapter Fourteen

Dual Pricing

As a consequence of the introduction of the euro, consumers will have to adopt new reference values for the goods and services they purchase. Providing their clients with good, clear information about the new prices will be an important marketing tool for firms that deal directly with the consumer, such as shops and banks. It is expected that shops will provide all kinds of information, such as conversion tables, calculators and dual pricing. Dual pricing will occur wherever and for as long as it is feasible and needed. The question could be raised whether it will be necessary to impose a legal obligation to display dual prices. Here opinions differ. This chapter gives the points of view of a retailer, a consumer organisation and a banker. It closes with some general remarks on pricing and marketing.

RETAILERS

Graham Harvey

The retail sector will play a pivotal role in the introduction of the euro because of the enormous range and number of monetary transactions involved in shopping, whether by cash, card or cheque. Both parties must be aware of the value of the transaction if the exchange is to be easily and quickly agreed. Any change in the unit of transaction therefore needs to be fully understood by both consumer and retailer.

Experience from cross-border shopping and tourism indicates that different currencies can be satisfactorily used in retail operations by most consumers. These transactions, however, are significantly slower than regular retailing, where delays would be critical. There is also evidence that most tourists translate prices back into their own national currency.

Experience of previous changes in monetary systems, for example, the UK's decimalisation in 1971, suggests that even modest changes take some time to be absorbed by the public. People need time to gain confidence in a new currency and to adapt to new coins and notes. Above all, they need time to become fluent in the use of a new currency before they are prepared to let go of the old system.

Consumer confidence and communication
The introduction of the euro will challenge consumer confidence as consumers are likely to have many questions and worries about the currency change. These may include concerns about maintaining their purchasing power, the transparency of prices, and the reliability of the conversion from old to new prices.

Before the euro can start circulating, it will be essential for these consumer concerns to be addressed in detailed campaigns by the European and national authorities to inform the citizens thoroughly about the advantages to be gained and the practical changes required. It is expected that the public authorities will be responsible for the general dissemination of basic information including conversion charts and tables. Retailers will be required to take part in the pre-information campaign through helping to produce official explanatory materials and by developing information tools adapted to their individual situations.

The range of possible information measures that could be made available by the retail sector includes:

> Conversion tables equating the euro to the national currency could be issued either by the national government or the retailer, adapted to meet the company's needs and marketing policy.

> Small special calculators: in the Netherlands a large number of devices similar to small calculators were distributed to help people switch to new telephone numbers; the idea would be useful for changing money between the national currency and euros (as no other function would be needed, the calculator would be very cheap).

> Price tables of preselected basic products: each point of sale could also display and/or distribute price tables, choosing products of most interest to the consumer as examples and showing prices in both currencies.

Dual-price labelling: the use of concurrent price indications showing both euro and national currency prices for all products, either on shelf-edge ticketing or on individual products, though expensive, is likely to be preferred by consumer organisations and the European Parliament.

In order to encourage consumer awareness and understanding of the euro and its exchange rates with established currencies, and to speed up acceptance by the public, it will be important to make conversion aids available well before the new currency is actually introduced. A planned and phased programme of introduction dates for the above listed aids would help to build up consumer knowledge. Here is a possible timetable, related to 'E-day' — the official launch date of the euro notes and coins:

Customer Aid	Introduction Date	Duration
Conversion tables	E-day minus 9 months	
Price tables	E-day minus 6 months	9 months
Pocket calculators	E-day minus 3 months	
Dual pricing	E-day minus 3 months	6 months

It is assumed that the conversion tables and pocket calculators would remain in use by the consumers as long as they consider necessary. Dual pricing would continue until original national currencies are withdrawn from use.

Dual pricing and the marketing of products
It is of paramount importance to the retail sector that consumer confidence in the reliability of price information is maintained throughout the introduction of the euro. Although costs will be involved in all these guidance measures, they will be supported by retailers who will wish to see a ready and speedy acceptance of the euro by the public at large.

The dual-pricing element will be the most expensive and burdensome role for retailers, particularly for small enterprises which sell large ranges of branded merchandise. Nevertheless, it is recognised as an essential element in the new currency information campaign.

Price information is given to the consumer in several ways, principally through shelf-edge tickets, individual pack pricing, or till receipts, and often via a combination of all three. Other methods include advertising, leaflets and window signs, though these are usually short-term and should incur no additional cost. For the majority of retailers, the preferred option will be the dual marking of shelf tickets which will bring the new price clearly to the consumers' attention on each occasion they make a purchase decision. For major retailers, especially those engaged in own-label merchandising, full-scale dual pricing of each product pack may be feasible and made part of a promotion aimed at offering a distinctive service to the consumer. Dual pricing of individual packs would be particularly challenging and difficult for the many small retail outlets and any legal requirement for this would threaten their economic viability.

Legislative and voluntary measures
If left to market forces, the choice of dual-pricing systems used by each retailer will reflect the company's marketing methods. Competition is extremely fierce in retailing and, as a result, companies constantly strive to improve the level of quality and the range of goods and services they offer. Consumer information and clear pricing are key elements of the service customers expect.

Supplying accurate and up-to-date information on the introduction of the euro, including methods of dual pricing, would fall into the category of customer service and would undoubtedly stimulate creative thinking among retailers on the best way to inform their customers. Presenting the information in a known house style could make the material user-friendly, more acceptable and more easily assimilated by the customer. A further advantage of presenting new currency information in corporate house style is that it would assist in the considerable training that will be required for all retail staff. The introduction of the euro will be significantly eased if all retail employees are well trained in its use before it enters the public domain and can thus help ease customer concern. The use of regular corporate-style training material will assist this.

On the other hand, a prescribed and legislative approach to dual pricing would have some advantages, including perhaps lower costs of origination of labels and ticketing and a standardisation of presentation techniques. These advantages, however, are likely to be reversed in practice because retailers could be obliged to install and use information systems alien to their particular store environments and inappropriate for their display techniques.

One particular concern about a legal format for dual pricing is that it would follow shortly after the enactment of the proposed EU directive on unit pricing. This directive, which is well advanced in the legislative process, makes it clear that, from 1999 onwards, a double indication of prices will have to be used for most products — that is, the selling price and the price per unit of measure (kg.,litre, etc). This means that where the euro dual pricing is to be implemented, four prices would have to be displayed for the majority of products. In cases of sales price promotion, the four old prices and the four new prices would have to be shown, a total of eight prices per product. This would lead to a plethora of figures which would confuse the consumer. Furthermore, to make sure that the prices were still legible, label and pack sizes would have to be significantly larger! One further point regarding a standardised and prescribed system is that it could take the place of established and proven labelling systems and so endanger the close relationship and understanding that exists between individual retail outlets and their customers.

Taking all these factors into account, it appears that a voluntary system of dual pricing, developed from existing price labelling systems, supported by both official conversion tables and individual conversion calculators, would be the best way to introduce the euro and the most effective way to establish consumer confidence quickly in the new currency.

CONSUMERS

Reine-Claude Mader

The introduction of the euro causes natural apprehension to consumers, even if they are in favour of it as a principle. Consumers will be afraid of losing their accustomed references for their transactions and managing their budgets — plus the threat of price increases.

Double price tagging is clearly the answer, but there are questions about its duration, the terms of its implementation and whether it should be compulsory. Double tagging will have an essential pedagogical role to ease the transition to the euro. It must be implemented during a long enough period, letting consumers stay in touch with their national currency, without falling into the trap of only calculating in their own currency. In our view, the duration of double tagging must be for a significant period of time, one year at least, with a follow-up lasting several months. That period would have the advantage of covering an annual cycle of a normal household budget.

Double tagging should not be limited to the prices of products and services. Consumers need to establish a link between their income and outgoings. The pedagogical approach must be integrated by applying dual pricing to salaries, retirement pensions, administrative payments, social security, taxes, sundry allowances and subsidies, bills, repayment of loans and mortgages, deposit books, savings accounts and bank statements. This exercise requires the modification of national legislation according to an overall EU framework.

The prime objective is to get consumers and citizens to approve the transition to the euro, and it is important to remember that a majority of EU citizens have never used a currency other than their own. Dual pricing is too sensitive a problem to leave to the retailers, and official harmonisation is required. Special attention must also be paid to needs of the vulnerable — the elderly, the disabled and the poorly sighted.

Nobody should remain indifferent to the outcome of the debate about whether or not to make dual pricing compulsory. Consumer organisations must make themselves heard; and the public authorities and professionals must find hard and fast solutions.

BANKERS

Pascale Valent

Dual pricing will play an essential role in familiarising the general public with the new currency. Consumer associations also see it as a means of ensuring that distribution channels do not take advantage of the currency change to increase their prices.

A certain number of instruments, such as public debt securities and exchange rates, will be quoted in euros starting in 1999 (Phase B). The Paris stock exchange plans to quote all securities in euros. Clearly, there will be a need to display their equivalents in national currency until such time as those currencies cease to exist. But if dual pricing were to be made made mandatory, this should apply only to the period after the introduction of euro notes and coins (Phase C). Moreover, there could ultimately be a need to extend the period of dual pricing beyond the date when the national currencies are demonetised and withdrawn from circulation, in order to satisfy public need.

Regulations governing dual pricing

There is considerable controversy about the issue of whether dual pricing should be made a legal obligation. If it is made obligatory, then it should be carried out uniformly throughout all member states in order to avoid creating distortions in competition. Dual pricing will be the primary means by which the general public will be able to familiarise itself with the scale of values in euros. Consumer associations are in favour of it, seeking to create a legal framework for the need for clear, informative price indications. Salespeople are not against the principle of dual pricing, yet they stress that detailed, restrictive legislation could run counter to the desired objective and prove both very costly and ineffective.

In any event, as dual pricing will ultimately become indispensable for proper consumer information, companies, including banks, are spontaneously gearing up to make dual pricing a feature of their sales strategy. Major retailers, anxious to jump on to the timetable for the introduction of the euro and seeking to give themselves a European image, have launched 'euro weeks' (as the Centre Leclerc supermarkets in France did in October 1996), during which they have displayed prices in both national currency and euros and allowed customers to pay for purchases in either national currency or metal euro tokens purchased at a price set by the distributor. These initiatives have the advantage of showing that the public can easily adopt a new scale of values, even in simulation. They have the disadvantage of potentially causing the public to mistake the fake money used in the simulation for the real currency which the euro will ultimately become. As questionable as these simulations may be from the standpoint of monetary orthodoxy, they demonstrate the extent to which companies will be tempted to include dual pricing in their marketing efforts.

Major retailers already consider dual pricing to be absolutely essential with respect to their customers. Very few small retailers and merchants, such as proprietors of luxury boutiques, can conceivably take the time to explain the mechanism of translating their national currency prices into euros to their customers. Banks are however gearing up to prepare their customers for receiving information in two currencies, though they do not believe they will be able to avoid a campaign of more personalised explanations once the first euro denominated bank statements make their appearance.

In those member states where prices are governed by detailed regulations, dual pricing, whether obligatory or not, will need to have established computation rules and schedules. The application of euro exchange rates will raise a certain number of problems which only the legal systems may be able to settle by means of judgments or agreements.

Banks and dual pricing
Banks will have no specific problem with displaying their fees and commissions in both national currency and euros. The same does not hold true, however, for presenting statements of account. Conceivably, either the balance could be translated, or each transaction could be presented in national currency and euros. Irrespective of its high cost, the second solution should be avoided.

There is a difference between translating the sum of several amounts and adding up individual amounts each of which has been translated and rounded off to the nearest hundredth. The example that follows illustrates the arithmetic. Let us assume a euro denominated account showing six transactions, as shown in the table, with a euro-Ffr exchange rate of 6.40408 (the franc's current central rate against the ecu). Using the first calculation method, the sum of the euro amounts, translated into francs, is equal to Ffr 47,678.38. The bank's computer obviously comes up with the same result if it begins by translating each amount into francs and then adding them up. However, if the second column showed the customer each of the amounts translated into francs and then rounded off to the nearest centime, the sum of the rounded off figures would come to 47,678.37 French francs.

Bank's translation (euros)	Customer's calculation (francs)
1,281.00	8,203.63
+ 1,465.00	+ 9,381.98
+ 1,893.00	+ 12,122.92
+ 1,743.00	+ 11,162.31
+ 567.00	+ 3,631.11
+ 496.00	+ 3,176.42
7,445.00	
x 6.40408	
Ffr 47,678.38	Ffr 47,678.37

As this one centime discrepancy is the result of nothing more than the accumulation of rounding off discrepancies, banks would clearly prefer to issue statements of account showing only one column of transactions with only the balance translated into the other currency. Dual pricing in national currency and euros would continue to play a pedagogical role, as each statement of account would give the customer the exact amount of his assets both in national currency and in euros. This would also help to eliminate one cause of unfounded disputes.

SOME REMARKS ON PRICING

Sammy van Tuyll

Price setting policy is an important marketing tool. Here, four points are made about pricing policies in the transition to the euro.

The first is about dual pricing, which has been discussed previously. It goes without saying that whenever a price is shown in euros as well as in national currency so as to give a reference value to the customer, the prices should be related to each other at the official conversion rate. Rounding should be done according to the official rounding rules as described in Chapter Eight, which is rounding to the nearest value. Not to apply the fixed conversion rate and rounding rules would be to mislead the consumer. In addition, it should be made crystal clear to the customer which price is in which currency.

A situation in which the customer thinks he buys a DM priced article, but eventually has to settle a euro price (nearly twice as much), should be avoided.

Secondly, there is often no unambiguous one to one relationship between prices in euro and national currency. This is particularly true for currencies where the smallest unit is smaller than the euro cent. The table below shows the result of converting a DM price into euro at the fixed conversion rate (here the ecu rate as of 22 November 1996 is taken as the hypothetical conversion rate) and converting the rounded euro prices back into DM. In almost half the cases the price is different from the original DM price. Showing a dual price of DM 0.05 and euro 0.03 is right when starting from a DM price, but wrong when you depart from the euro price. In the latter case it should be euro 0.03 and DM 0.06. It follows that one cannot always achieve neutral dual pricing, and the customer should be told which price is the dominant price and which the derived one.

The third point is that for marketing purposes too it is necessary to make the distinction between dominant and derived prices. Prices are often expressed in terms of so-called psychological prices, such as BEF 99 instead of BEF 100. The table below shows the conversion of psychological prices from BEF into euro. The result after rounding is generally not 'psychological'. New psychological prices will therefore have to be set, which may lead to a small price decrease or increase, compared to the national currency price. Marketing considerations will suggest a choice between a dominant and a derived currency.

The fourth point concerns the often expressed fears that the changeover to the euro will lead to price increases. As the last table shows, the setting of new psychological prices will lead to small price increases as well as decreases. But these will probably cancel each other out. Here consumer organisations will have an important role to play in making price surveys and informing the public about which firms maintained their overall price level, or even slightly decreased it, and which firms used the changeover to increase their prices. Clearly, where prices are usually very flexible, such as meat, fruit and vegetables, and change several times a day, it will not be possible to regulate the changeover of prices. Market forces, enhanced by price surveys, will make sure that overall price increases do not occur.

DUAL PRICING AT FIXED RATES

Conversion rate: 1 euro = 1.93182 DM

price in DM	converted to euro	euro price rounded	converted to DM	DM price rounded
0.01	0.005176	0.01	0.019318	0.02
0.02	0.010353	0.01	0.019318	0.02
0.03	0.015529	0.02	0.038636	0.04
0.04	0.020706	0.02	0.038636	0.04
0.05	0.025882	0.03	0.057955	0.06
0.06	0.031059	0.03	0.057955	0.06
0.07	0.036235	0.04	0.077273	0.08
0.08	0.041412	0.04	0.077273	0.08
0.09	0.046588	0.05	0.096591	0.10
0.10	0.051765	0.05	0.096591	0.10
0.11	0.056941	0.06	0.115909	0.12
0.12	0.062118	0.06	0.115909	0.12
0.13	0.067294	0.07	0.135227	0.14
0.14	0.072471	0.07	0.135227	0.14
0.15	0.077647	0.08	0.154546	0.15
0.16	0.082823	0.08	0.154546	0.15
0.17	0.088	0.09	0.173864	0 . 1 7
0.18	0.093176	0.09	0.173864	0.17

PSYCHOLOGICAL PRICING IN BELGIAN FRANCS AND IN EURO
Conversion rate 1 euro = BEF 39,0456

BEF	euros	new 'psychological' price in euro
29	0,74	0,69 or 0,79
39	1,00	0,99
49	1,25	1,19 or 1,29
59	1,51	1,49
69	1,77	1,79
79	2,02	1,99
89	2,28	2,29
99	2,54	2,59
199	5,10	5,09
299	7,66	7,69

Chapter Fifteen

Problems with Vending Machines

Steve Green

Coin production of the euro is due to start in 1998 and, by the beginning of 2002 following three years of continuous coin production, the changeover from national currency to the euro will begin. The length of the transition period is the subject of much debate. Proposals range from a six-month transition period to an overnight 'big bang', in the same way as UK decimalisation in 1971. The length of this transition period and the capability of the vending machine at the time to be truly 'euro-ready' will be critical to the ongoing profitability of the vending operator.

This paper considers the challenges which will face the vending operator to ensure that the currency changeover is managed in the most efficient way.

The current number of vending machines in Europe, for countries with an installed base of more than 50,000 machines, is as follows :

1996 installed base of vending machines (thousands)								
	DE	FR	UK	ES	IT	NL	BE	Other	Total
Drink	320	475	240	165	215	120	51	98	1,684
Food	50	215	150	1	15	7	6	17	462
Cigarettes	800	0	150	120	0	5	8	11	1,094
Total	1,170	690	540	286	230	132	65	126	3,240

It can be safely assumed that by the year 2002, the total number of vending machines requiring upgrade will exceed four million, as the rate of new machine placements currently exceed old machine retirements by around 5% per year on average in most countries.

Changeover Sequence

The changeover from national to single currency will typically follow four steps:

- Programme the euro coins into the coin mechanism ;

- Enable acceptance of the euro coins and implement internal credit conversion for euros to national currency,

- Modify the change payout on the coin mechanism and the external credit display,

- Disable the acceptance of the national coins.

For coin mechanisms supplied before the euro coins are made available in volume, the first step will take place during 1999-2001; the later steps will have to take place during the transition period in 2002. In more detail, these steps are as follows :

First, the acceptance of the euro coins will have to be programmed into the coin mechanism. Coin mechanisms supplied post-1998 are likely to have the euro coins already pre-programmed and therefore this step will not be necessary. For coin mechanisms supplied before this time, however, the programming will need to take place. This could be done at any time from mid-1998 when the coins are made available in volume to coin mechanism suppliers. For simplicity, the average life of a vending machine and coin mechanism is approximately ten years. It is clear that by the year 2002, approximately 70% of the field-base will not have the euro coins pre-programmed, and will require this first step to have been actioned during the preceding three years.

Second, the euro coins will have to be enabled — that is, 'switched on'. The optimum time for this will be either just before or on the actual day of introduction. At this point also, the vending machine will need to internally convert euros into national currency value and display credit appropriately. On non-MDB machines (Multi-Drop Bus, the current recommended interface standard for new vending machines), this conversion will need to be carried out within the coin mechanism.

Third, the coin change-giver will need to be modified to provide change in euros. It is important not to take this action too early as the number of euro coins in circulation will be small and unlikely to be able to keep the change-giver replenished. This would lead to lost sales. Modify too late, with the same result. The optimum time is likely to be within a four to eight week band within the six-month overall transition period. This means that a typical vending machine operator with around 800 machines, will need to convert vending machines at a rate of 100-200 per week in order to minimise losses. At this point also, price displays will need to be converted to euros and the national currency (which will still be accepted as legal) will have to be internally converted in value to euros and displayed as credit appropriately.

Finally, the acceptance of the original national coins will need to be disabled. The optimum time for this will clearly be on the day of withdrawal.

Changeover Scenarios

The following graph considers a hypothetical six-month transition scenario (where the initial rate of euro introduction to the final rate of national currency withdrawal is rapid), and illustrates how these four steps fit into the transition period.

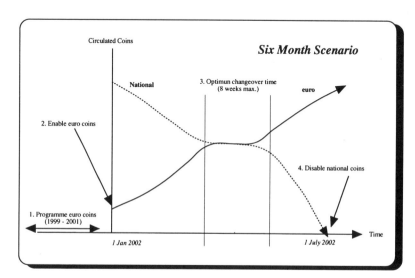

In all possible transition scenarios, the key challenge facing the vending operator will be in determining the optimum times to reconfigure the vending machine. Either too soon or too late will lead to lost sales.

The 'big bang' scenario will potentially be very costly for the vending operator and very damaging for the vending industry as a whole. Ideally, all machines will need to be converted on the day of changeover which, for most medium and large sized operators will be impractical. Sales will be lost due to machines not taking euros and non-legal national currency will be accepted by the machine.

It is likely that, if faced with the big bang, vending operators will be forced into fully modifying most of their machines early in preparation for the changeover day. This will lead to lost sales. These losses might be reduced if the euro coins are pre-circulated (maybe eight weeks before the changeover day), effectively as tokens. The European Vending Association (EVA), after much consideration, has recommended to the European Commission that the transition period should be six months.

Challenges and requirements

The challenges facing the vending operator comprise timing (to minimise loss in sales revenue), logistics (to minimise investment cost), and technical (to minimise specialist training costs). All operating companies will require a simple, fast, high quality method of upgrading the vending machine on site.

With a four to eight week changeover period, many large operators will be faced with the challenge of simply getting it done in time. First, the ability to modify the existing payment system (coin mechanism, bill acceptor or card reader) without removing it from the machine will be essential to avoid the need for expensive 'float stock' which might otherwise be needed if the payment system had to be returned to the depot. In addition, the ability not only to accept the new currency but also to pay back euro coins as change will be required. Again it is essential that the required changes to the coin mechanism can be made without removing the payment system from the machine and without the need for specially trained technical staff.

All operating companies will wish to avoid the cost of specialist training for this exercise. Simplicity will be the key as the intention will be that the route fillers (those who visit the vending machine on a regular basis to restock it, to collect cash and to carry out cleaning and basic maintenance) will carry out the upgrade as part of their routine visits. If the technical requirements for the upgrade are complex, then it will be unlikely that enough specialist vending machine technicians will be available to carry out the upgrade within the required time.

Other areas of the vending operation affected include the payment mechanism (coin changegiver, coin acceptor, bill acceptor, card reader, Vending Machine Controller (VMC), vending machine price and credit display, spare parts, audit system (where used), cash collection, coin counting, sorting and banking, accounting, administration and logistics.

The 'euro-ready' vending machine

The key to the truly 'euro-ready' vending machine lies within the payment system. As most coin mechanisms from 1999 onwards will have the euro coins programmed into memory as standard, the key factor will become the speed and simplicity with which the vending machine can be converted to display prices and credit and to give change in euros. The required coin mechanism will be one capable of accepting all versions of euro coins plus national currency, of converting monetary values into a clear display for the consumer and of providing change for the transaction in the appropriate currency.

Providing change in both currencies at the same time will add unnecessary complexity to the vending operation. This concept is impractical and will not be necessary if the changeover is managed correctly. The vending machine which best helps the operator to overcome the challenge will be the one which can be upgraded on-site by unskilled personnel. Any on-site upgrades will have to be fast, discrete and of factory standard.

Chapter Sixteen

Logistics of Cash Conversion

Françoise Billon

The European System of Central Banks will be responsible for circulating euro denominated bank notes and removing national currency denominated bank notes from circulation. Coins, however, will be circulated by the national central banks of the individual member states.

The more opportunity the public has to use euros, the more adapted it will become. The frequency of making cash payments will not be a negative factor, provided that the public can obtain euros as readily as national currency. In contrast, the public continues to hesitate over infrequently used notes and coins. In France for example, 100 franc coins are hoarded and rarely used for payment, and 500 franc notes are occasionally refused.

The introduction of the euro will be based on systems already organised within each member state for distributing currency to economic agents. The scope of the problem depends, above all, on the size of the country: bank notes and coins in circulation in Germany represent 300 times the value of cash in circulation in Luxembourg. It also depends on personal habits: the typical German uses ten times more cash than his Dutch counterpart and twice as much as the average Frenchman. Cash (bank notes and coins) accounts for less than 9% of payment instruments (M1 monetary aggregate) in the UK; 15% in France, Italy, and Luxembourg; 25% in the Netherlands, Belgium, Spain, and Portugal; and 30% in Germany. In countries where wages are frequently paid in cash, notes and coins play an even greater role, representing nearly 40% of M1 in Ireland and Austria, and more than 50% of M1 in Greece

In order to avoid upsetting popular habits, the European Monetary Institute has decided that there will be eight bank note denominations (5, 10, 20, 50, 100, 200, and 500 euros) and eight coin denominations (1 and 2 euros; 1, 2, 5, 10, 20, and 50 cents). A German will use 5 euro bills where he would otherwise have used 5

AVERAGE PER CAPITA VALUE OF NOTES AND
COINS IN CIRCULATION IN 1994

Belgium	988
Denmark	737
Germany	1,441
Greece	563
Spain	1,152
France	671
Ireland	584
Italy	863
Luxembourg	981
Netherlands	148
Austria	1,229
Portugal	409
Finland	343
Sweden	853
United Kingdom	414
European average	915

or 10 mark bills. Cash machines will issue 50 euro bills, where they had previously issued 100 mark or 100,000 lira bills. In France, where the most common bills are 100 and 200 francs, cash machines will have to issue 10 and 20 euro notes. In Sweden, 500 euro bills will have to be issued, as Swedes today use 10,000 kronor bills. Each member state will have to prepare its own practical system for introducing the single European currency, provided it complies with market practices in terms of standardisation.

The physical introduction of the euro will take place in two stages: circulation of the new currency starting on E-day and withdrawal of national currencies, until their complete elimination on L-day. Euros will coexist side by side with national currencies during the interim. In this chapter, we will not consider the legal controversy surrounding the continued circulation of national currencies as legal tender during that period; we will simply look at logistic and organisational issues.

Circulation of euros on E-day

Two traps will have to be avoided: panic exchanges of cash holdings in banks as soon as euros are circulated, on the one hand, and complete indifference to the euro until L-day, when all EMU national currencies have been removed from circulation, on the other. E-day will have to be preceded by an information campaign that is sufficiently long and intensive to ensure that euro-denominated bank notes and coins are readily identifiable by merchants and the public. Visual displays in each member state with euro notes and coins are displayed alongside national currency, arranged according to a euro-determined value scale, could facilitate their identification. If the idea of printing a national symbol on the first generation of euro-denominated bank notes were chosen, the national symbol would have to be sufficiently discreet as to avoid its being an obstacle to the use of the notes in any of the other participating countries, and especially to avoid the obligation of returning used bills to their country of origin.

The cross-border circulation of cash is limited today, but it will probably grow with the advent of the single European currency. Staff training in banks and retail stores will be very important, because employees will be called upon to answer consumers' questions. There is also a specific problem of training large numbers of temporary and part-time staff employed in retailing. Training efforts will have to be stepped up in the week preceding the circulation of the new cash.

Countries have always avoided making monetary changes on 1 January because training sessions for employees would have to be intensified during the last week of December, which is the busiest period of the year (inventories, account cut-offs, preparations for and the holding of year-end sales). Experience has shown that the best time for making monetary changes is between mid-February and mid-March.[1]

National central banks will circulate the notes according to demand. Presumably, the well established procedures for supplying the economy with national currency will not have to be changed for the introduction of the euro among commercial banks, companies, or particularly retail stores. Their capacities will have to be readjusted, however, because the size of present-day supply channels is determined by the replacement of used bills. The conversion to be made will be of a completely different scope. Even if it is spread out over a number of weeks, it will require the creation of masses of cash, whose shipment and warehousing will raise serious space and security problems, and the central banks will have to share the responsibility for these problems with the commercial banks. It will also be necessary to change the financial methods used to create cash reserves, to be debited from the accounts of institutions that acquire cash from the central bank, because their amount will be equal to all the cash in circulation.

Any entity that must issue cash to the public will have to have prepared its staff very carefully for the event. Though banks and other financial institutions are the first to come to mind, other cash issuers will include post offices, tax and social administrations, and hospitals, as well as a number of companies that still pay staff wages in cash.

In order to avoid queuing in banks for exchanging cash, euros will be distributed primarily in three ways:

•cash withdrawals from commercial bank teller windows;

•supply of bank notes and coins to companies and retailers;

•cash withdrawals from automatic teller machines (ATMs).

In the first two cases, bank and post office employees will have been trained to attract customer attention to the new scale of values of the euro denominated bank notes and coins. They will probably have to answer questions concerning exchange rates, the manner in which figures are rounded off, and the disappearance of the smallest subsidiary currency units, such as 1, 2 and 5 groschen in Austria; 1 and 2 pence in Ireland; 1 drachma in Greece; 1 escudo in Portugal; 1 penni in Finland. (France has already eliminated its 1 centime coin, and Italy has done the same with its 10 lira coin.) Store and company cashiers will face the same questions.

The preparation of cash and money changing machines will raise the need for two types of operations: mechanical and electronic. Mechanical operations, corresponding to physical distribution, will necessitate adjustments that will vary in duration according to the compatibility of the new bank notes and coins with the old ones. Most manufacturers feel that adjustments can be completed in two years once they are informed of the physical characteristics of the euros. Electronic operations on cash machines and money changing machines, involving the recognition and monitoring of bank notes and coins, raise other problems. Their manufacturers believe they are in a position to prepare new machines in time, once they have been informed of the characteristics of the euros (probably starting in 1998).

Yet it will take more than a few days, or even a few weeks, to put millions of machines into operation. The most urgent task would seem to be to adjust the fleet of cash machines, which is smaller. As the fleet of cash machines is constantly being modernised, and the machines themselves updated, it has been recommended that all new cash machines installed starting in 1999 be capable of distributing euros.

Cash machines distributing euros will be linked to euro denominated accounting and reporting channels. Cash withdrawals will be debited from accounts that are also denominated in euros. Modifying cash machines would seem to be the final stage in the changeover of consumer transaction processing channels to euros.

	Cash machines	Cash cards (000s)
Belgium	3,170	8,912
Denmark	741	2,825
Germany	29,400	81,418
Greece	1,617	667
Spain	23,425	32,352
France	20,533	22,812
Ireland	862	3,359
Italy	18,672	12,936
Luxembourg	3,663	359
Netherlands	4,998	13,988
Austria	4,998	3,512
Portugal	3,329	5,291
Finland	4,255	2,269
Sweden	2,281	6,037
UK	19,500	69,800
Total	**141,444**	**266,537**

The period of dual currency circulation

Due to the amount of cash involved, its sociological and geographical dispersion, and the amount of time needed to adjust (or replace) the millions of machines designed to operate with bank notes and coins, it was considered impossible to execute the currency changeover in a matter of days. A period of up to six months has been planned, during which time national currencies will continue to circulate alongside euros. Independently of the legal aspects, which are discussed in Chapter Eight, dual currency circulation raises serious practical problems, similar to those involving the foreign exchange of bank notes, but on an entirely different scale: involving all payment instruments, as opposed to the relatively small number of payments made by non-residents in neighbouring countries.

Holding cash and making cash payments in two currencies doubles the risks involved (theft, destruction). It would necessitate dual accounting, in national currency and euros. Transactions processed in national currency will have to be translated according to the irrevocably fixed conversion rate in order to reconcile national currency denominated accounts with euro denominated accounts. Two methods may be used for this purpose: economic agents who handle large numbers of operations on a daily basis (banks, large corporations) plan to translate all national currency operations as they occur. Others plan to carry out translations of daily, weekly, or monthly balances, depending on their management needs. The first method will prove the more expensive, as it will only be used for a short period of time, and it should thus be avoided wherever possible. This would seem to be possible, and desirable, at least in retailing.

As the period of dual circulation must end with the rapid and complete elimination of national currencies, the suggestion could be made that retailers give change exclusively in euros starting on E-day. This would save the cost of dual accounting of inflows and outflows, not to mention the fact that, in many cases, it will be physically and ergonomically difficult, if not impossible in some stores, to install and manage side-by-side cash registers.[2] At the end of each day, national currency inflows would simply be added to euro inflows, which will be recorded directly. The question also arises as to how retailers would give change in euros and national currency to customers paying in national currency. This apparently complex operation could be handled in one of two ways:

The first method should be avoided, as change due in national currency varies, its euro value must be calculated each time, and the amount will not necessarily be accurate. Rounded off figures are always subject to disagreement, and cashiers will have to justify their operations to customers each time.

The second method is more convenient. The euro value of each national currency denominated bank note will be irrevocably established in 1999. This will settle the issue of rounded off amounts. Cashiers (and consumers) could immediately tell how much change they are to receive in euros. Retailers would avoid having to maintain dual accounting, by accounting for payments made in national currency as euros, and depositing the national currency cash with their banks, which will make the conversions and credit their accounts in euros. Another appreciable advantage of this method is to accelerate the elimination of national currency denominated cash. Similarly, government administrations and public services could accelerate the process of switching over to the euro. They make many cash payments involving, for example, welfare benefits, postage stamps, and revenue stamps. These entities must be among the first to familiarise the general public with the new currency. Though they will continue to accept payment in national currency, they should be required to make payment only in euros starting on E-day.

PAYMENT IN NATIONAL CURRENCY WITH CHANGE GIVEN IN EUROS	
1st Method	*2nd Method*
payment in national currency	payment in national currency
- amount due (in national currency)	x exchange rate
= change due (in national currency)	= value of national currency in euros
x exchange rate	- amount due in euros
= change given in euros	**= change given in euros**

Demonetisation of National Currency Denominated Bank Notes and Coins to be Completed on L-Day

It may now be assumed that, starting from the first date of issue of euro denominated bank notes and coins, banks will be forbidden to provide their customers with national currency; they will only be able to issue euros. However, until L-day, they will be able to accept national currency either for immediate conversion into euros (bank notes and coins) or for deposit and credit of the euro exchange value to their accounts.

This raises the issue over whether a limit should be placed on the number of euro-denominated bank notes a branch should be authorised to issue per day or per week to each individual (requests from business customers will be less random). Today, anyone may change any amount of notes into another currency at any branch. Experience has shown that bank branches can run out of funds in the event of unexpected demand. Though this is inconsequential in the case of foreign currency operations, it would have a negative impact when replacing national currencies with euros. Interbank cooperation will have to be organised in such a way that no one institution finds itself incapable of making conversions.

As usual, retailers will play the role of concentration, accepting national currency payments from their customers (recorded in their accounts) and presenting the accumulated national currency cash to their banks, which will convert it into euros for deposit in their accounts. Judging by past experience, merchants will probably place regular orders for the quantities of euro notes and coins they need for the conduct of their business; they will be less inclined than banks to make immediate conversions of national currency cash into euros.

Banks, which will play a key role, will have to put together numerous teams of agents capable of efficiently handling bank note exchange operations for the duration of the exchange period: advising depositors, providing explanations, counting bank notes submitted for deposit, conversion, counting bank notes issued in exchange, and crediting accounts. This activity will supplement everyday branch activity. The geographical breakdown of these teams may have to differ appreciably from that of other agents.

The question of whether this extra work load can be remunerated has yet to be answered. There is a consensus around the idea that the issue should be left up to competitive forces, with each institution allowed to set its own rates. Even in those member states with the most restrictive banking regulations, central banks would not rule out the remuneration of the conversion service provided that such remuneration is justified. Financial institutions will then have to establish the cost of verifying, sorting, and storing the cash, and then shipping it to a central destination for destruction.

---

[1] 31 March 1960: introduction of the new French franc; 15 February 1971: decimalisation of the pound sterling and creation of new pence; 2 July 1990: demonetisation of the ostmark.

[2] The cost of adapting equipment (new euro cash registers and terminals) has been estimated at more than ecu 4000 per till on the assumption that merchants must give change either in euros or national currency at the customer's wish (entailing the manipulation of two currencies and the creation of two cash tills per cash register). The cost falls to less than ecu 400 per till, excluding staff trading, if change is given exclusively in euros.

Chapter Seventeen

Case Study: A Commercial Bank

Peter Wolf-Köppen

As monetary policy will be conducted in euros from 1 January 1999, banks have to be ready by that date to do at least a part of their operations in euro. The Commerzbank set up a steering committee on EMU as early as summer 1995. This committee is dealing with all questions concerning the conversion to the euro. EMU activities at the Commerzbank are related to three issues:

1. Technical and organisational preparations. These mainly concern data processing and software, hardware like cash dispensers, bank statement printers, ATM (Automatic Teller Machines) and cash counting machines.

2. The impacts of EMU on banking business, in particular, the direct and indirect effects on our business units as well as the opportunities and risks in competition.

3. Communication on different levels, both internal and external, with employees, customers and federations, by organising meetings with customers, training seminars and communicating with the general public.

It is in the field of data processing programmes that we need to concentrate our initial work. The adjustment of the hardware is not as urgent as the software. Here we have to consider the extent to which we can combine new hardware (or adjusted hardware) with expenditure on new equipment.

Schedule for the technical and organisational conversion
At present we are still at the stage of making examinations, plans and estimates. But at the beginning of 1997, Commerzbank as well as other German banks will start changing their information technology programmes. From this time, the changeover activities will actually cost money. We believe, at Commerzbank, that around 80 to 90% of

all software conversion activities will have to be carried out in 1997 and 1998, probably with a small overhang remaining for 1999. During Phase B, more and more transactions will be handled in euro, but our IT changeover activities can then be allowed a small pause. There will be a second but smaller thrust around 2001-02 when the remaining customer accounts and stocks will have to be converted and euro denominated notes and coins are to be issued.

Why is the conversion of IT program so time consuming and complicated? Some may say that all that needs to be done is to make sure that the fields which now show the national currency contain the new currency in the future, which must be very simple. Others, though, point to the fact that nearly all IT programs are implicated in one way or another. And as we have no big bang, but a gradual transition, interim solutions must be created for a three-year period, thus complicating matters. The truth lies somewhere in between. At Commerzbank one third of all programmes are concerned to a lesser or greater extent. And it is also true that nearly all products are effected by the conversion. Commerzbank has subdivided its IT activities into different projects. This, of course, will be handled differently by each bank depending on what is considered most appropriate.

Commerzbank's principles for the IT changeover strategy
The steering committee on EMU developed three principles for the IT conversion. Although they are defined for the technical conversion, they do have a clear connection with the business policy of Commerzbank:

1. Multicurrency systems for all products. This relates to the question of which products will be offered only in national currency during the changeover period and which products will be offered in both currencies. In Germany, all banks seem to be prepared to offer (and settle) most products in DM and euro, although there is great uncertainty whether German customers (private and corporate) will actually demand services denominated in euro to any great extent. Commerzbank decided as follows:

- To make all necessary technical preparations so that we are able to offer and settle all products in both currencies when the changeover period begins (although our private customer department is not sure whether they can or will actually offer all products).

- At the time of the changeover we will try to bring all products into a multicurrency system. This is already the case for some products, but must still be made for others. The additional costs will be kept within reasonable limits and has been accounted for. With the changeover to multicurrency systems we will try to maintain flexibility.

Based on the principle 'no compulsion, no prohibition', we expect the new currency to be used in most areas of banking business, as is shown in the table.

USE OF THE DM AND/OR EURO DURING CHANGEOVER PERIOD (PHASE B)

Banks	Payments/interbank	**Only Euro**
	Payments/customers	**DM and Euro**
Capital markets	Stock Exchange	
Money markets	Equities	**Mostly Euro**
Forex dealing	Bonds	
	Money and Forex dealing	**Euro**
Corporates Institutionals	Basic currency	**DM or Euro**
	Invoicing	**DM or Euro**
	Payments	**DM and Euro**
	Investments/Credits	**DM and Euro**
Private customers	Payments	
	Accounts	**DM and Euro**
	Deposits	
	Credits	

There are, however, doubts about whether private customers will demand euro products to a large extent. It must be asked if private customers will convert their current accounts to the euro, especially when German banks will offer account statements on which the euro-amount is printed for the customer's information anyway, and also whether customers will request a savings deposit or credit in euros as long as notes and coins in euros are not available? On the other hand, we expect that, due to the 'no compulsion, no prohibition' idea, there will be competition among banks with euro products for private and of course corporate customers. At least it is believed today that no major bank or bank group can afford to disregard customer demand.

2. Priorities for customer service. This concerns the division of priorities between customer services and internal data processing. Special importance in connection with the IT changeover activities is attached to the interface between customer and bank, and the Commerzbank views this as a top priority. The customer will receive DM or euro data on paper or by electronic banking. This is the first time that the new currency will become visible to the customer. The print-output is, therefore, very important.

The internal 'comfort' of data processing has a lower priority. For example, the conversion of historical data shall be done in a very restrictive manner. We are planning to convert historical data only subsequently and if required. Besides, all necessary conversions will be made through a central converter, thus obviating the need for the installation of numerous programmes and avoiding converter-chaos.

3. Basic Currency, Home Currency, Account Currency. Our third principle is that we will continue to keep the whole data file in one currency during the transition period. This means that there will be no parallel operations in both currencies. Nevertheless, the subject data file is somewhat more complicated than it may look. First of all, each bank must decide whether it will continue its accounting and controlling in national currency or whether it will switch to the euro entirely during the transition period. This is also one of the first and most important questions which corporate bodies have to answer.

It is necessary to define what we call the basic currency for the whole bank and for the group. This is the currency used for all accounting and controlling operations. Customer exposure is also expressed in the basic currency. Therefore all limits, as far as they are denominated in a currency, and all collateral must be shown in the basic currency. Whether a bank (or a company) chooses the national currency or the euro during the changeover period is a question of which currency is considered to be the most appropriate. There are four reasons why Commerzbank intends to keep the DM as basic currency till the end of the year 2001:

- The greater part of business, especially with private and corporate clients, will still have to be transacted in national currency.

- The public sector, including the revenue office will probably stick to the DM during these three years. It may even be the case that public authorities cannot accept reports or notifications in euro.

- We are anxious to avoid excessive stress in IT conversion activities before Phase C.
- Last but not least there is a certain, small risk that EMU might be cancelled or postponed.

But even if the bank as a whole sticks to the DM as basic currency, it might be possible that a single business unit switches to the euro for its 'home currency'. For certain business activities, such as treasury, forex, equities, bonds and asset management, it could be more appropriate to switch to the euro as home currency in order to accustom employees to think only in terms of the euro. If the basic currency and home currency differ, it will be necessary to ensure that the data flow for profit and loss accounting, controlling and risk management are converted back to the national currency. These problems should not be too big but one has to build the interfaces to avoid converter-chaos.

Things look somewhat different as regards the so-called account currency of the customers. The data processing programmes should allow customers to choose their account currency and to switch to the other at any time. Banks must keep in mind that customers may not switch all their activities (current account, deposits, credits, securities account and so on) to the new currency at the same time. The criterion 'account currency' should depend on the product rather than on the customer. For instance, what of a customer who has a current account in DM, a deposit in euro and a credit in dollars? The total exposure of this customer must, of course, be expressed in the basic currency, either the national currency or the euro.

Payments and current account as key to the customer
In Germany, attention has been paid to this area of changeover preparations at a very early stage because no distinction is made between retail and wholesale payments systems. It was therefore agreed to convert the whole payment system between the banks to the euro at the beginning of Stage Three. A key to the German solution is that a customer can give payment orders both in national currency and in euro, irrespective of the denomination of his current account. The sender's bank transmits the data file through the clearing system with the amount expressed in both currencies and quoting the original currency. The recipient bank looks for the account currency of the recipient customer and chooses the correct amount from the data file.

The scenario described here concerning the conversion of payment systems applies only to Germany. The solutions in other participating countries might be different.

Current state of IT preparations in Germany

The German Banking Association has carried out good work in the preparation of IT for the changeover. With the help of its member banks they produced a best-selling manual and checklist for all private banks. But it forms only a basis for preparations: each bank has to make its own concrete decisions according to its own special data-processing programs.

The technical and organisational preparations of the big German banks are more or less on the same level. The Commerzbank has already done much preparatory work in 1996. We investigated whether the IT programs were affected by EMU. It was found that this was the case for nearly a third of all existing IT programs. The requirement for adjustments was roughly defined and a time-schedule prepared. A matter of great importance for us was the future manpower demand, because our IT capacities are always heavily utilised, and it became more and more evident that it would be time-consuming and complicated to change some of the very old programs. We decided therefore to create totally new programs to cater for EMU. We improved our specification and reduced the forecast risk from 100% to nearly 30%. At present we think that the change of IT software within the next five years could be carried out with a capacity of 250 man-years. We have also involved our branches abroad, other subsidiaries and some affiliated companies into our preparations.

At the Commerzbank we calculate that the adjustment of software (internal and external) will cost approximately DM 100-120 m within five years. The greater part of these costs are integrated with normal IT budgets, which will increase significantly as a result of EMU. Up to now we have not calculated the expenses for hardware because the time when this will become relevant is still rather distant. All in all we calculate the total costs to be about DM 150-200 m.

Fundamentally we have to expect that high capital investments will be necessary in electronic banking and foreign payment systems because EMU will accelerate the competition in technology-driven products. On the other hand we hope that the improvement of old systems and the installation of new ones will help the firm to increase its productivity.

Chapter Eighteen

Case Study: A Multinational Company

Walter Dilewyns

In contrast to financial institutions, who need to be prepared, industrial and trade organisations have the benefit of the time allotted to Phases B and C, and this at their own pace, adapted to their own circumstances. Indeed, the reasons to delay the process are multifarious. Sceptical arguments are not easy to counter.

So the first question a company must answer is: what are the economics justifying an early start or an acceleration in the changeover timetable? There are many arguments and advantages in favour of starting with the changeover process:

- Starting in time offers the opportunity to incorporate the necessary changes smoothly in other projects, which have to be done anyway, in order to reduce costs and lessen opposition.

- Clients or suppliers may want to deal in euros.

- The introduction of the euro offers a firm a unique possibility to present itself as a 'European company' and in doing so strengthen its competitive position.

- A company may want to enjoy as soon as possible the advantages that simplified procedures in, say, cash management and consolidation, can bring.

- In many organisations, the changeover is looked at as a problem and a big burden. In increasing the awareness of the opportunities that the single currency will bring, uncertainty and related 'soft-cost' can be removed.

- In the switch-over process, strategic decisions will have to be taken as early as possible, but in view of their far-reaching consequences, hasty decisions should be avoided.

It is clear that the conceptual framework of the changeover process will be influenced by the specific set of goals a particular company wants to achieve in accelerating the implementation.

Appoint a change-agent

One of the first things the board of directors of a company should do, probably after a limited study, is to appoint a 'euro-change-agent'. He or she will act as a catalyst and assume responsibility for managing and coordinating the changeover process throughout the entire company. As the source of the problem is monetary or financial by nature and also rather technical, the finance director or treasurer will probably be the right person for the job.

The task is not easy as the introduction of the single currency is clearly a process of change, and it is common knowledge that people are averse to change as it leads to uncertainty, conflicting points of view and stress. The main tool in the changeover process will be information and communication. The information should be to the point, reduce uncertainty and induce reflection about the concrete impact of the introduction of the euro. Information pollution should be avoided in order to save time and money and above all to keep the attention focused.

Steering committee

Once enough information is available, the agent should initiate the switch-over process. The best way to do so is to establish a steering committee or 'euro-platform', encompassing the driving forces from all the different functions of the business involved. Here we already have to ask which business functions are affected and to what extent? First in line, of course, stand finance and accounting, and with them the linking and supporting information systems. But marketing, logistics, controlling, personnel and legal departments will all be affected. All business functions are involved, and have several dimensions. The problems or necessary changes encountered in, for example, accounting, can be quite different at headquarters level from those encountered in affiliates. Headquarters may probably already have multi-currency software, whereas affiliates are unlikely to do so. Dual pricing will be a hotter topic for a sales organisation, which is nearer to the customer than headquarters, where the focus is more on transfer pricing.

The global mission of the steering committee can be summarised as the development of an overall switch-over concept and the initiation, coordination and controlling of the implementation of the necessary modifications.

The steering committee should be the driving force behind working groups for each function. It will be up to these groups to:

- make an analysis of the effects and implications that the introduction of the euro will have in their area;
- specify and describe the changes required;
- develop a switch-over concept;
- implement the necessary adaptations.

Definition of the problem
A lot of analytical work will have to be done. An attempt to define the problem and to put it in the right perspective should clearly be the starting point. The changeover to a single currency confronts us with:

- the birth of a new reference currency;
- the coexistence of two currencies in each state involved for a period of up to 42 months, due to the fact that the 'Big Bang' scenario has been dropped;
- in the end, the elimination of the 'local' currency.

The coexistence of the old currency and the euro during the transition period obviously adds another dimension to the changeover. The introduction cannot be classified as a mere conversion problem, as the way to handle two denominations of the same currency has to be figured out. Having such a three-step scenario in mind one should try to determine what is changing and how it is changing. Four basic types of consideration come to mind. The first are technical in nature, with the following common denominators:

- one time conversion and evaluation problems of, for instance, historical data, of assets and liabilities, cost accounting, wages, pension fund reserves;
- recurring conversion problems due to the need, for one reason or another, to dispose of particular data expressed in the old currency and in euro;
- adaptation problems of, for example, the internal electronic data processing systems and applications, of the communication systems with third parties, sales conditions, reporting;

- modification of planning and budgeting procedures.

A second type of consideration concerns communication. A prerequisite for a good preparation of the changeover is the availability of clear and timely information. A good communication strategy in this matter will diminish the costs involved. Attention has to be paid to the following :

- all those concerned should be fully informed on the changes in order to enable them to identify the eventual needs for conversion, adaptation, modification and to work out the necessary preparatory measures;
- communication vis-à-vis third parties, which are not only suppliers and customers but also banks, public institutions, shareholders, unions, etc., in view of the settlement of the affairs in hand;
- internally, the personnel should be informed on the implications concerning their financial relationship with the company, wages, social security, pension fund reserves, and so on.

A third point regarding corporate strategy is the need for negotiation. In the first instance, a lot will depend on the specific position and plan of the company. Is it in a situation to enforce the use of the euro on suppliers? The story will be quite different vis-à-vis clients. Besides, one should bear in mind that third parties might impose the use of the euro upon the company.

Finally one should think about the strategic implications and opportunities. The introduction of the euro is not only a matter of technical adaptations, but an opportunity to optimise organisational structure.

Evolution of the different tasks

Throughout the different changeover phases which have been officially determined, the different tasks appear to be as follows:

Phase A1

Before the decision on the starting date and participating countries, which is scheduled for early 1998, the emphasis will lie on the following:

- legal adaptation, modification or completion of the long term contracts in order to allow an easy conversion to the new currency;

- internal communication strategy aimed at the supply of information that stimulates reflection on the consequences of the changeover for the business function involved;
- screening of the different plans of action with regard to the switch-over;
- identification in detail of the elements that have to be adapted and if a legal framework is needed or desired, the communication of this to the authorities concerned;
- after identification and regulation, start implementation process;
- start external communication regarding the company's intentions and wishes regarding the introduction of the euro.

Phase A2

After the determination of the first group of participating countries:

- the implementation will become more concrete and gain momentum;
- if the decision to go full into the euro from 1 January 1999 has been made, a tactical and practical plan to organise the initial transition will have to be worked out, as some particular or critical elements may not be known;
- intensification of the external and internal communication strategy.

Phase B

- start of the EMU and market-driven changeover in the non-cash area;
- further transformation of the processes that were not converted from day one;
- give assistance to retail-outlets in solving problems due to dual pricing and the non-availability of euro cash;
- working out a strategy for the evolution and possible entry of the 'pre-ins' in this period.

Phase C

- replacement of notes and coins and completion of the currency changeover by 2002 at the latest.

Chapter Nineteen

Case Study: Small and Medium-Sized Enterprises

Many small and medium enterprises do not have the resources to cope with the current exchange rate uncertainty. The establishment of EMU will create new opportunities for them.

A PORTUGUESE PLASTICS FIRM

António José Pires

The Fábrica Leiriense de Plásticos S.A., was founded in 1956. Since the adoption of the tubular extrusion process in 1969 our main product has become the plastic film used in industry, agriculture and construction. When Portugal entered the European Community in 1986 the company was small, with a production volume of PTE 900 million and around 200 employees, and it aimed almost exclusively at the national market.

Due to the restricted size of this market the company basically owed its development in the first thirty years to a strategy of import substitution, involving six different ways of processing plastic material. The productivity of the company at the end of this period was on the low side: only 30% of the average productivity of other similar companies in the region. The management structure was rudimentary: supervision was limited to a central accounting department with an average delay of three months.

The 200 or so employees were not organised in a formal structure. As the company then had existed for thirty years, the average age of the employees was 45. Besides, 10% were illiterate and 65% had received only primary education. At this time, with the prospect of Portugal entering the EC and opening national market to competition from other common market countries, the future did not look very promising. The time had come to reflect upon and anticipate the consequences of the EC accession and prepare the company for the future.

Preparing for the single market

At the end of 1986, after a period of profound reflection on different aspects of the functioning of our company, a plan was made for a reorganisation of the firm that would allow it to survive in the common market in the medium term. It involved the following points of action and goals:

- concentration on the development of two of our activities: the manufacture of plastic film and the recycling of plastic waste material;

- improvement of the level of organisation, including the use of information technology, the reorganisation of the production process and the improvement of the technological capacity;

- penetration into external markets.

This led to the following results in 1986-89:

- sales went from PTE 994 million to PTE 1,852 million and exports increased from PTE 128 million to 458 million;

- the number of employees was reduced from 177 to 154; productivity more than doubled

- an industrial accounting system was introduced;

- in 1988 the factory started operating around the clock, in four shifts, which allowed us to dispose of 50% of the machinery and reduce energy consumption by 30%;

After this first phase of the reorganisation process the results were analysed and a plan formulated for the 1989-93 involving a further improvement of the company performance, professional training of all our employees, discontinuation of non-competitive products and a search for merger partners. Leiriense España was established and W. Wooderson was acquired to operate the distribution in the Spanish and English markets. Moreover, an agreement was reached with a Belgian company to represent their line of products in the Iberian market. In addition, several measures were taken to improve productivity, such as contracting out of transport, improving the factory layout, installing new administrative units and further automatisation. The number of employees was reduced to 87 in 1993, their productivity being nearly four times the 1987 level.

Preparing for the single currency

With the introduction of the single currency we can certainly expect further economic integration between the countries that form the European Union. One of the last barriers to the free movement of goods and services, the local currencies and the possibility for each country to protect its market by monetary and fiscal policy, will disappear. Companies functioning within the borders of the Union will not have to bother with exchange matters any more. The purchase and sale prices will all be expressed in euros, which will undoubtedly facilitate the commercial and financial management of the majority of the companies, and in particular the SMEs, who to a large extent do not have sufficient financial, human and technical resources to operate in an environment of exchange uncertainties.

Another factor to take into account is that fifteen or so national markets, all more or less protected, will evolve into one single market without barriers. Moreover, in the medium term, as a result of the GATT treaties, the single market will become more and more accessible to outside countries and in particular to the Asian countries who possess capital, have access to technology and can produce at extremely low prices.

Consequently, the globalisation of markets, the disappearance of exchange policy measures as instruments to influence external competitiveness, the creation of possible advantages of scale for certain sectors of industry, the continuous pressure on price levels and the increasing importance of factors such as quality, marketing and computerisation systems are elements which determine the competitive position of companies. In this scenario creativity plays a fundamental role in finding solutions, often defying the conventional approach, which have the advantage of being aimed at a specific enterprise/market context. Obviously the application of such solutions requires a heightened capacity to absorb changes on the organisational, methodological and cultural front.

Can the SMEs find reasons to compete in such a larger market? The yes to this question will have to go hand-in-hand with a package of structural measures such as the attainment of critical size, a strong accent on quality, the diversification of the supply of goods adapting them to specific needs of the different segments of the targeted market, the development of distribution channels, a strong reliance on computer and communication systems and the acquiring of credibility on the market scene.

Opportunities for SMEs

The cost of financing will go down, which will allow more investment and lower expenses for SMEs, which are traditionally short of capital. Greater competition will lead to lower purchase prices. The larger size of the markets will increase trade opportunities. It is very important that the elimination of exchange risks within the European Union will enable a large expansion of the activities of the SMEs. Competition will lead to an improvement of resource allocation, which will create new opportunities, especially for SMEs, as larger companies will tend to refocus their enterprise on their core business.

A FINNISH SUPERMARKET

Jouko Kuisma

This supermarket in Finland has 1500 square metres of selling space, ten checkouts, a range of 5000 articles and an annual turnover of ecu 10 m. It has an advanced information system including scanning and electronic fund transfer at the point of sale (EFTPoS). The opening hours are from 09.00 to 20.00 (Monday to Friday), from 08.00 to 18.00 on Saturday, from 11.00 to 18.00 on Sunday. Before the introduction of the euro, the legislation of the opening hours will probably become more liberal than it is today. There are 11,000 customers per week, half of whom shop on Friday and Saturday. At the moment, 40% of the purchases are paid by cards: by 2001 this will probably rise to more than 50%.

Software changes in time

In an advanced supermarket, there is no need for changing hardware, but there will be changes in the software. The required software exists already and costs between ecu 1000 and 3000. It is necessary to plan and order the modifications well before the third phase, as in the last few weeks the suppliers will definitely have many orders, which suggests that there will be a shortage of time and the price of software will be higher.

Customer information on a voluntary basis: dual pricing in larger stores

Customer information also has to be planned well in advance. Approximately three months before the notes and coins are launched, the store will start printing dual price labels to be put on the shelf edges. FIM will still be the main price, and the euro price will be printed in a smaller size. The computer will count the euro prices through a conversion program. The store will also display conversion tables, price comparison tables, leaflets etc. whilst the starting day for showing both currencies depends on the competition.

It is very important that dual pricing is not made compulsory. The larger stores have technical possibilities of producing two prices, but the costs of dual pricing covering the whole range of goods is too high compared to the short period when it will be needed, because there are other much cheaper, and equally efficient, ways of teaching customers. In particular, smaller food stores and speciality stores will have great problems in implementing compulsory dual pricing. The authorities have to understand that all extra costs raising consumer prices have to be avoided. Competition will definitely solve all information problems the consumers may have.

Requirements for notes and coins

The supermarket, as well as other big food store companies, have large customer volumes, which require standardised, rational working methods and solutions. For the euro, this means that:

- the notes have to differ clearly from each other by colour, to avoid mistakes in their recognition;

- all notes have to be of the same size, which helps handling and counting (in supermarkets, counting machines are commonly used and have to be adapted to the new notes);

- the size of the coins should reflect their value logically: the bigger the value, the bigger the coin.

The staff responsible for cashier activities have to be trained in a half-day seminar about two to three months before the store starts working with the euro. The cashiers will get in-store training during the final few weeks. The training requires printed material, probably produced by the banks and the trade organisations.

The in-store training cannot be done during the Christmas season. For this and other purposes it is very inconvenient and expensive to launch the euro cash on 1 January. The retail trade, especially the bigger food stores, would like to start in the middle of the week, outside of all seasons. A very suitable day would be Thursday 1 November 2001.

Handling of purchases at the checkouts
As the price data will have been switched from FIM to euros on the night before the big day, the cash registers will print each price on the receipt in euros. Dual pricing is not possible on each individual item, but the total sum of the purchase will then be shown in FIM through the conversion.

The customer will then be asked whether they want to pay by card or cash. Card payments will be sent to the banks or card companies in euros only. If the customer uses cash, they can pay either in euros or in FIM during the changeover period. If the payment is in euros, the notes and coins will be put in the till as usual, and the change will be given in euros. The cash register will show the amount of change. If the payment is in FIM, the money will be put into a separate safety box attached to the checkout desk. This is a box where one can put money in but not take it out. The change will be given only in euros. As all the stores will follow this principle, the changeover period will more or less be over in one month. During the changeover period, the amount of change needed will be larger than normal. The stores are not willing to pay for the extra costs as the whole operation is not caused by changes in their business but by government decisions.

The handling of customers will slow down and produce queues
The possibility of paying either in euros or FIM will slow down the speed of serving customers. At present, the average time at the checkout is two minutes, but during the changeover period we estimate two and a half minutes. As there are about 2000 customers in the store on Friday between 15.00 and 20.00, this means that during those five busiest hours 1000 minutes (16 hours 40 minutes) more of cashiers' work is needed if we want to maintain the same level of service. With three checkouts, 15 hours would be needed; but there is not that much unused capacity as eight or nine of the ten are already in use on Friday night. The number of customers and the

situation on Saturday between 10.00 and 15.00 is approximately the same.

It can already be predicted that only the biggest stores will be able to maintain their service level and avoid longer queues. Of course using all available checkouts will increase costs. In the aforementioned example, if the extra 15 hours' work were possible on Friday and Saturday, it would cost 30 x 15 = euro 450 a week and euro 1800 a month, which is a 2.4% rise in personnel costs (which are about 45% of total costs). The shorter the changeover period, the less expensive it will be to the stores and their customers, and the small stores would then not lose their customers to the big stores with shorter queues.

After closing the store
In counting the money, there are two possibilities. Some stores count the balance themselves, some buy this service from the banks. In both cases, two currencies have to be kept separately during the procedure. As the euro notes and coins are different from the FIM notes and coins, the counting machines have to be adjusted from euros to FIM and back, or two separate counting machines are needed. This will require more time and incur costs. If the counting is done manually, the required extra time is much longer.

As the FIM notes are gathered into the safety cash boxes, it may be necessary to empty these boxes more often than usual. This means increased money transfers inside the store and increased security requirements.

When the money is taken to the bank, the bank will convert the FIM into euros when transferring it to the retailer's account. The bank should not charge anything for this conversion nor for the extra costs of counting two currencies during the changeover period, as these transactions are based on government decisions.

When the changeover period is over
After a certain time, in the food stores after approximately one month, but hopefully within six months, this project will be over. The price data is in euros, no conversions will be made, and no more FIMs will be accepted. If the price information has included dual pricing on a voluntary basis, some of the price labels might be kept on the shelves and then gradually taken away, as soon as the store learns that

the customers have got used to the euro. Everything will work as it used to with the old national currency.

A medium sized supermarket is flexible enough to prepare for the euro and to get along during the changeover period without remarkable costs, if:

- the starting day is a working day outside the high seasons;

- the price marking and other customer information can be solved without compulsory dual price regulations, letting the competition force stores to find practical, inexpensive and informative solutions;

- change is given in euros only, thus speeding up the vacuuming of the national currency from the market.

Chapter Twenty

Case Study: Non-Cash Handling SMEs

Andreas Henkel

An SME which does not sell to consumers will be much affected by the question of when to changeover to the euro. Big international industries may intend to change over soon after 1 January 1999, whereas SMEs engaged in retail and similar businesses will change over around 1 January 2002, because the currency in circulation will determine the basis of almost all their accounting systems. A non-cash handling SME will find itself in a situation somewhere between these two extremes.

Purchasing

For example, a paper processing SME will buy its raw materials from international firms within the paper industry, which will tend to change over at an early stage of Phase B (KNP-Leykam, for example). The SME will probably have to agree to pay in euros soon after 1999. If there are only a few of these purchases, this will not constitute a reason for an early changeover in parts of the accounting system. Banks are expected to provide for an automatic conversion of payments if the bank account of the SME is still denominated in the national currency, and the supplier's bank account is already denominated in euro. An additional module to convert payments might be sufficient to avoid an early changeover. But the SME might have to be prepared to enter price talks with its main suppliers, because these suppliers might be forced to recalculate their whole range of products to arrive at psychological or more practical prices for certain products. The relevant data bases have to be checked and possibly changed. Long-term contracts concerning securities will also have to be checked in time and possibly be completed by a euro clause. The SME has to consider the possibility of out-sourcing some parts of its products to profit from economies of scale.

Sales and marketing

A paper processing SME normally has many customers (perhaps 10,000), ranging from wholesale and retail trade to individual, mainly industrial, customers. Some of these customers are also expected to use the euro soon after 1999. If the SME is to be forced to calculate and invoice in euros by its main business partners, this could constitute a reason for an early change over for the SME. So at least this part of the accounting system, which is dealing with calculation, offers, invoices and collection proceedings, could be converted at an earlier stage.

The SME also has to consider the necessity of drawing up new or double price lists for its customers. In many sectors of the economy, price lists are not published on 1 January. This applies especially to toys, furniture and cars. These non-cash handling producers and traders will therefore have to find an interim solution for this problem. Maybe the SME will have to repackage its products to reach new psychological prices or new customers. If necessary, a new marketing and advertising strategy has to be developed, taking into account new information needs of the consumers and business partners, even if the SME is not selling to consumers directly.

The SME has to think of redesigning its terms of business, harmonising its terms of payment and possibly converting its backlog of orders. As EMU will cause more competition, the SME must also try to win new customers in the whole EMU market, not only in its former home market. Wholesale trade and mail-order businesses will strengthen their market position, so the SME will also have to review its business links and its marketing strategy. Paper processing SMEs will be winners of EMU in any case, because many other enterprises will need new forms, business papers, price lists and packaging material and, of course, new promotional material for their advertising campaigns.

Controlling and financing

The SME has to set up a detailed business plan for the changeover to fix internal responsibilities. This should prove to be a useful tool for planning and budgeting the necessary investments caused by EMU. The rhythm for investments should be adapted to the timetable of EMU. Medium and long-term plans as well as characteristic figures could already be converted into euros. Financial management has to be redesigned according to the expected interest rate level. Relations with banks should grow closer to prepare for the changes in the payment systems and credit transactions. An SME with business contacts in many EMU countries will have to reconsider these links and possibly reduce them in order to save money.

Accounting and taxes

The SME has to define the time to change over, bearing in mind that the national tax authorities will most likely be the last of all public authorities to change, because double accounting would cause them severe trouble. So the SME has to take into account that the balance sheet in particular has to be drawn up in the national currency until the end of 2001 and all tax payments will also be in the national currency until then. Only the part of the accounting system dealing with calculation and invoicing could reasonably be converted at an earlier stage. The SME has to check if double accounting, at least in some parts of the accounting system will become necessary, especially in Phase C, or if this can be avoided by special, additional conversion software. Assessment problems caused by the changeover have to be reviewed concerning long term contracts and credits, futures trading, other foreign currency debts and credits. If the fiscal year does not begin on 1 January, the SME should possibly alter this point of time.

As the fiscal and social authorities will change over only by the first half of 2002, the payroll accounting (including pay slips) should also be carried out in national currency until the beginning of 2002, although an early conversion would be possible, because the payments would be converted into the national currency by the banks, the bank accounts of the employees thereby remaining denominated in the national currency.

The SME should also take into account that a national regulation might force it to show net income in payslips in both currencies. In this case the SME will have to adapt payslip and also payroll accounting software. But the essential prerequisite for all these conversion processes is the timely preparation of financial regulations by national authorities (conversion of tax allowances into euros etc.) as well as the timely adaption of collective agreements to the changeover.

All these, sometimes minimal, changes have to be incorporated into the new accounting software. So the strategy to adapt all software and possibly hardware concerned with the needs of the changeover process becomes a central issue for the SME. The firm has to identify all the systems to be adapted for the use of the euro including the programs designed for statistical tasks. It should distinguish between systems developed by the SME, systems bought from the market and further developed by the SME and systems bought ready from the market. It should then contact the relevant software providers in order to get information about their changeover plans, and analyse the necessary and possible conversion needs in the external accounting systems as well as in the internal ones.

Following the setting up of a changeover strategy, the SME has to organise the changeover process (required manpower etc.) and provide an investment and financing plan for the years ahead, starting in 1997/98. These plans should take into consideration that obviously not all systems can be adapted at the same time, or at least not at the beginning of a fiscal year. The changeover plans also have to be harmonised with the overall investment strategy. Any SME which is now considering new investment or adaption of its software systems (for instance for the well-known problem of the turn of the millennium) should take into account all these conversion needs in order to minimise costs. Provisional investments should be avoided or at least postponed.

In order to be properly prepared, the SME should be aware of the fact that the software industry has clearly indicated that the changeover costs will not be incorporated in the normal upgrading contracts, but will be separately charged. The relevant industries expect years of high growth, obviously to be financed by their customers. As the minimising of costs should be in the centre of the efforts of all SMEs, solutions for groups of enterprises or whole sectors of the economy should be envisaged. This could be done by cooperation at the level of SMEs or by concerted actions at the level of professional associations. As a consequence, joint solutions would ease the pressure on firms to pass on the costs for the changeover to their customers.

Personnel

The personnel of the SME have to be prepared for the introduction of the euro. Evidently this is true for all the issues mentioned above: employees have to be able to answer the questions of customers and business partners and to communicate the changeover strategy of their enterprise. As soon as the business plan is ready (responsibility of top management), the employees have to be informed and trained for their new tasks. Joint solutions should be envisaged: in cooperation with social partners, joint training modules could be developed according to the needs of the different sectors of the business community. But the employees are not only ambassadors of the enterprise, they themselves have to be informed by the management about the enterprise's changeover strategy. They need to be sure that the introduction of the euro does not leave them as losers. It is very important that the entrepreneur wins the confidence of employees not only regarding business strategy, but also so that they will not be disadvantaged by the euro. In particular, the wage policy of the SME has to be carefully designed and the payroll accounting should be made transparent for employees.

In detail, the following steps for the changeover strategy have to be envisaged, possibly in cooperation with the works councils: it should be clear from the beginning, that wages (and pensions) can only be paid in euros from the beginning of Phase C, because notes and coins will not be available before January 2002. But beforehand the tariffs of collective agreements have to be converted taking into account the official exchange rate and the rounding principles agreed at national or at EU level. All payments exceeding the tariffs must be converted too. The relevant databases and software have to be adapted feeding in the new euro figures per each single employee, if formulae cannot be easily applied. Income tax tables should be adapted by national authorities in order to facilitate the changeover of payroll accounting. As the personnel databases are used for many purposes, a parallel payroll accounting should not be ruled out. Wages of personnel employed in foreign countries and the possible implications of changes in tax-deductible travel expenses have to be checked. The reserves as well as the payments of pension funds have to be converted.

A working party or at least a high ranking person should be put in charge of identifying and analysing the changeover problems and coordinating the whole conversion process. The schedule and investment plans have to be fixed and rechecked according to the development of the legal environment and the markets. SMEs should also set up a reporting system to monitor and if necessary adapt the implementation of company strategy.

Chapter Twenty One

Case Study: A Retail Group

Louis Frère and Sophie Goblet

GIB, the leading Belgian distribution group is active in four sectors: supermarkets and hypermarkets (64% of turnover), DIY (20%), catering (8%) and specialised distribution (8%). In 1995,the turnover was BEF 232 bn. The GIB Group is not only active in Belgium (80% of turnover), but also in Europe (9%) and in the United States (11%).

If all goes according to plan, and if Belgium joins EMU from January 1999, the GIB Group will be operating in an environment which will be more favourable to its activities in the long term. However, the introduction of the single currency will have important implications in all areas, and will require many changes by the Group and its subsidiaries. The urgency and importance of these changes have led the GIB Group to prepare now for the introduction of the euro so as to maximise the advantages of EMU and to minimise the costs of the necessary changes.

The establishment of a euro working group

Under the responsibility of the division for finance and administration, a euro working group was formed in order to guide GIB and its subsidiaries throughout the various stages of introduction of the euro. The structure set up to consider the changeover, regroups heads of departments, representing the various functions (taxes, information systems, accounting) and their active branches (supermarket, hypermarket, DIY).

The objectives of the working group, while obviously set to evolve during the various stages of transition to EMU, are first of all to unravel the intricacies of the changeover to the single currency and to establish a list of sensitive areas and problems with which GIB will be faced. It also attempts to estimate the costs of the various solutions to be implemented before, during and after the transition period.

EuroCommerce (the retail, wholesale and international trade representation to the European Union), in a preliminary report on the impact of the transition to the euro on the commercial sector, has estimated the cost between 1 - 2% of annual turnover in the distribution sector. A first cost evaluation for the GIB Group should be finalised before the end of 1996.

At a later stage, the euro group will need to establish sub-groups according to the type of problem to be resolved in order to satisfy the specific and technical needs of departments concerned.

A multinational group

GIB Group, like all firms, will be confronted with certain difficulties during the various stages of the changeover to the euro, as follows:

- Adaptation and organisation of software: this crucial problem affects all department and all subsidiaries, and will involve heavy cost. However, a part of the cost could be shared with the IT project which aims to adapt the computer programs to the next millennium.

- Accounting operations during the transition period: the cheapest solution currently appears to be the treatment of the euro as an additional currency until the year 2002, the moment at which accounting will change over entirely to euro.

- Information requirements of current and retired employees.

- Communication with shareholders and suppliers.

- Miscellaneous: at the moment GIB does not need a financial rating (S & P, Moody's) to access the capital markets in Belgium; will the same apply when the euro is the sole currency? The firm must also check that the transition costs of our partners are not passed on.

At the moment these different problems are being studied by those responsible in the various areas, with their correspondents in other companies or with certain professional organisations.

A distribution firm

GIB, being active in many diverse areas of distribution, will moreover be confronted with problems specific to its sector of activity. Given its distribution activities, it is certain that the group's subsidiaries will not be able to change over completely to use the euro on 1 January 1999 and its clients will continue to use the Belgian franc until the end of Phase C (30 June 2002 at the latest).

Ideally, the duration of Phase C should be as short as possible in order to avoid the additional costs involved in dealing with two currencies and to minimise the risks of dual circulation. From an organisational viewpoint, 1 January is not the most convenient date for the distribution sector, given the onset of the New Year sales, and coming immediately after the Christmas holiday. Moreover, even though 1 January is regularly defended in order to facilitate the accountancy of the financial markets, this is not true for GIB whose financial year ends on 31 January. The uncertainties which remain about the dates and duration of the various stages of the transition to the euro are delaying the decision-making process concerning the measures to be taken, and risk increasing the associated costs.

The problems of dual circulation are principally of an organisational and physical nature. Moreover, their associated costs may rapidly become significant as they often involve additional hours worked without value added. One approach is to install double tills (involving investment for every till in every shop), implying double petty cash (double the money gaining no interest) and double counting (twice the work for one operation). This solution, associated with the possibility of giving change only in euros, allows a rapid reduction in the use of the Belgian franc and rapid introduction of the euro. Another approach is to separate BEF and euro tills, and progressively shift all tills to the euro by the end of Phase C. This solution would avoid the cost associated with the dual till option and change would be given in the same currency as the payment. However, this approach would considerably slow down the elimination of the Belgian franc.

Other problems concern the adaptation of insurance to cover higher amounts of money in circulation in the shops. The weight and volume of the euro will probably differ from the weight and volume of the franc (more coins and less notes). Will the number of transporters required need to be increased? The handling and transport of coins being more expensive, costs will rise. From the moment the euro is put into circulation, it will be necessary to ensure sufficient quantities of all notes and coins. Shops will have to adapt their cash orders accordingly. Should one envisage being paid in scriptural euro (cheque or electronic fund transfer (EFT) terminal) from 1999? This would involve planning to install conversion keys on tills by 1999, and more importantly, necessitate the training of shop personnel from then on. The technical characteristics of the euro (weight and volume) will determine the required changes in security systems (safes, transport bags); and shopping trolleys and change machines will have to be adapted.

Dual pricing

As yet, no decision has been taken which would legally impose the labelling of prices in both currencies and it is not certain whether such an obligation would be imposed. If such a decision would be taken, it would be important to know for how long it would exist. These two elements are essential for determining the choices GIB will make inadapting its systems and methods of price labelling. While it is obvious that it is in the Group's interest to inform its clients clearly of the changes brought about by the introduction of the euro, it is equally clear that dual labelling on the shelves is not the most efficient way to achieve this.

In fact, such a system, added to the requirement to label items per unit, would in certain cases involve the need for four labels (total price and unit price) and eight labels in the case of promotions or sales. The consumer would doubtless be more confused than enlightened by such a multiplicity of prices. Furthermore, if GIB is obliged to resort to dual labelling, the costs will be so high that there is little chance that the Group could envisage yet another budget for extra information purposes. On the other hand, if there is no obligation for dual pricing, market forces will ensure that the information of the consumer is optimal, and the means used will be more efficient.

The printing of folders, advertisements and above all catalogues (annual), will require very particular attention and very careful preparation. When the conversion rate is fixed, it will be necessary to choose the currency to be used for promotional or psychological pricing quickly — for example, a price of BEF 99 (euro 2.53) or euro 2.49 (BEF 97)? Information printed on the receipt will also be very useful, although the printing speed and the format of the receipt will have to be adapted. Particular care will have to be given to the various fidelity card systems. The 'points' cards linked to amounts spent in

BEF will have to be changed and linked instead to euros; in the same way, amounts spent in order to qualify for reduction cards will have to be adapted.

Even if it is still premature to talk in clearly defined terms about the commercial policies which will come into play with the introduction of the euro, one can certainly expect new opportunities for GIB which will lead to new activities in order to increase profit margins. Communication with customers will also be extremely important in order to minimise their discontent and help them to adapt to the euro. It is, however, too early to describe with any precision what means of communication will be proposed (conversion tables, basic products, simplified calculators).

Even if GIB, given its size, has the means to prepare in good time for the transition to the euro, it is very likely that some of its franchise outlets are currently less aware of the problems involved, and the Group will need to offer them efficient and rapid support.

Belgium is currently preparing the changeover to the single currency, but not many people are considering the implications and repercussions of the transition with regard to their own work. GIB is therefore attempting to draw the attention of management to the probable consequences of the introduction of the euro in the various areas, explaining the various stages involved, and the possible consequences of the transition in their respective fields. Beyond the problem of communications, the Group is also preparing to train its personnel, who will be confronted directly with use of the euro from 1999, principally the financial and accounting departments, but also the buyers who, from 1999, may have to negotiate with many of their suppliers in euro. The second step will be the training of those staff members who will be in direct contact with clients, under the responsibility of the various firms concerned. This represents long-term work, as it concerns the vast majority of personnel working in shops.

Conclusions

The non-exhaustive list of problems outlined above highlights the imminence, the complexity and the size of the problems related to the introduction of the euro. The euro represents costs and investments in the short term, which will be recovered in the long term by improved prospects and the eventual creation of an environment economically favourable to GIB and its subsidiaries.

The GIB Group has already started preparing the transition to EMU so as to minimise the changeover costs and to plan the additional costs the Group will incur in the coming years. More than a monetary problem, the introduction of the euro will concern, in one way or another, the entire workforce and all areas of the Group. This overview also illustrates the importance of the decisions which need to be taken by the European institutions and national authorities. Indeed, uncertainties with regard to dates and the duration of the various phases prevent the company from establishing a planning strategy, from evaluating the costs and from making choices. Other more technical uncertainties, such as the size and weight of the euro are also barriers to decision making which would allow GIB to proceed smoothly towards the single currency.

Chapter Twenty Two

Case Study: Challenge for Public Administration

Pierre Duquesne

European public administrations became aware only recently of the major changes which the introduction of the single currency will entail for them and of their decisive role in facilitating is unprecedented transition. In certain countries, the first efforts go back no further than spring 1995 (notably with the publication of the Green Paper by the Commission, the first official document published on this subject), but preparations mostly date from that autumn and the organisation of a working group 'on the adaptation of public administrations to the use of the single currency' by the Monetary Committee of the European Union. This permitted a first exchange of views and experiences whose results prompted the Madrid European Council in December to adopt the following conclusions within the definition of its 'reference scenario for the changeover to the single currency':

> 'New tradable public debt will be issued in Euro by the participating Member States as from 1 January 1999. ... The generalisation of the use of the Euro for public sector operations will occur in all participating Member States at the latest when the Euro bank notes and coins are fully introduced. The time frame will be laid down in Community legislation and might leave some freedom to individual Member States. The public authorities are invited to set in hand the arrangements for planning the adaptation of their administration to the Euro'.

The public administrations of the member states have since embarked on a process to transfer their entire transactions from their national currencies to the euro within a period of six years, which does not seem excessive. Even apart from their statutory tasks, it is already becoming clear that the economic and financial weight of public administrations will be crucial for the successful introduction of the euro.

The statutory tasks of public administrations prompt them to carry out extensive internal preparations which will be completed with the introduction of euro bank notes and coins. Even if the public administrations can and must prepare themselves for euro-denominated transactions from 1999 onwards, their changeover will mainly take place when euro-denominated cash is introduced.

Amendment of laws and regulations referring to national currencies may seem to consist of a stock-taking process. However, given that it may involve compiling an inventory of several thousand texts, it may be advisable to adopt a single horizontal law providing for replacement of the national currency's name by the name 'euro'. But this may turn out to be more complex than it seems: it will not only be necessary to replace the name of the national currency but also to change minimum or maximum values in the national currency which will have become meaningless. Moreover, in addition to national administrations, this work concerns EU institutions and local administrations. Lastly, it not only affects the legal texts themselves but also a host of administrative brochures, documents and forms.

The changeover of taxation will occur officially with the introduction of coins and notes. The nature of the various taxes does not call for different changeover dates. However, a distinction could be made between the different categories of operators concerned. In fact, major companies which pay company tax or VAT already want to be able to pay these taxes in euros before the euro becomes obligatory for private taxpayers. (Households may well want to do the same if, as becomes more and more likely, banks decide to offer euro-denominated bank accounts.) In other words, public administration needs to be prepared to accept this type of payment during the transition period.

It is naturally more reserved towards accepting tax returns in the single currency (except for customs), which would require enterprises to keep euro-denominated accounting and private citizens to receive euro-denominated statements from their financial intermediaries and employers. So far, only the Belgian authorities have publicly taken a position, in a document entitled *Lignes de force financières du schéma national de place*. It advocates the right of Belgian subjects to use either the franc or the euro both for documents sent to the tax and social security administrations and for their payment, with the cost of conversion being borne by the financial institutions. Belgium has the freedom to choose accounting currency.

The changeover of public accounting to the euro would in all likelihood occur only at the time when notes and coins are introduced. This is in fact the case in Belgium, whose tax and social security administration will continue to manage its internal information flows in francs during the transition period. Generally speaking, management costs and technical complications make it impossible to keep two segregated accounting systems. Conversely, starting in 1999, public accounting should be able to record payments and revenue in euros, even if the volume of such transactions will still be limited and mostly concern subscription, redemption and payment of interest on euro-denominated tradable public debt. Various accounting solutions are available to cope with these constraints, notably the French proposal to keep a 'master' account in the national currency and a 'mirror' account in euros. A delicate technical problem, which, while not limited to public accounting, is of special importance in this area because of the amounts involved, lies in the rules on rounded figures, regulated by the text on the euro's legal status.

The budget of member states will not change before the introduction of euro cash. However, for educational reasons, certain member states have announced plans to present their budget in both their own currency and the single currency from 1999 onwards. The introduction of euro-denominated coins and notes will therefore be the factor sparking most of the administrative changeover as well as the final expression of the sovereign prerogatives of states and central banks. While certain technical problems (notably the materials used for coins) and political issues (the size of the distinctive national sign to be displayed on one of the two sides) remain to be settled, most work has been done: a final selection of artists entrusted with the monetary signs should be made in the months ahead.

Operational preparations
At first fragmented and limited to analysis, preparations have quickly become operational and relatively coordinated. In its conclusions, the round table on the euro organised by the Commission in January 1996 suggested the creation of a *national steering structure* in each member state (whose membership would represent the players concerned: administrations, central bank, private operators, consumers, etc.), the adoption of a changeover plan by each administration and

the implementation of a closely coordinated information campaign at European level.

So far, the players concerned by the introduction of the euro have not been systematically brought together in a single structure. Generally, the national central bank manages relations with banking and financial operators while the ministry of finance manages relations with other ministries, local administration and public agencies. It is not certain whether such a single structure is currently feasible or even desirable, given that the host of initiatives do not necessarily lend themselves to centralisation.

Originally limited to financial administration, awareness work and preparations have since spread to all national as well as local administrations, various local authorities and public agencies, notably social security organisations. In France, for example, a circular sent by the prime minister in March 1996 invited each minister to form a permanent working group whose chairman would be the outside contact for all problems generated by the changeover to the euro. A task force at the Ministry of the Economy and Finance, charged with the changeover of the administration to the euro, ensures inter-ministerial coordination. These plenary groups have themselves set up specialised subgroups, dealing with legal, computer, communication and training problems. They also meet at inter-ministerial level. At local level, the changeover is monitored by a steering committee chaired by the prefect of the Department.

Inventory efforts are gradually succeeded by efforts to set deadlines and costs. Given that member states estimate the average time needed to prepare for the changeover at three to four years, ongoing analysis must obviously be wrapped up quickly. Adaptation of computer programs (also obliged to cope with the switch to the next millennium) should definitely start before 1999 and some changes should already start now. Even listing the necessary adjustments is a time-consuming task. Computer applications are connected by many links. It is essential to implement a transverse structure to monitor the project. While certain tasks will probably be subcontracted to computer service providers, such companies will most likely be overloaded.

There is little doubt that the changeover in each member state (whether with a centralised or federal government structure) will simultaneously affect the various levels of public administration, which often use similar and even identical management and accounting rules (although intermediate administration which is not in direct contact with the public could change over at an earlier date). By contrast, it remains uncertain whether it is advisable to coordinate at EU level the changeover of the public administrations of the member states that have entered the third stage. The conclusions of the Madrid summit call for a degree of coordination (which could notably be useful in specific sectors with strong interfaces between member states, such as social security, customs and VAT). On the other hand, respect for the principle of subsidiarity naturally requires independence of national actions.

Management of public debt
The economic and financial weight of public administration invests it with a strategic role in the changeover to the euro, which will largely determine the success of the operation. The issuance of new tradable public debt in euro as from 1 January 1999 will be a decisive factor, reflecting the belief of the EMU states in the irreversibility of the process, and having significant consequences for the operation of the capital markets.

The euro-denominated long rate market will have several sovereign benchmark issuers distinguished by premiums which measure the country risk as well as the liquidity of national markets: even if issuing policy continues to be defined nationally, it will have to factor in this natural classification. This will naturally increase competition between sovereign issuers to attract national and foreign investors, and prompt issuers to gear the type and liquidity of securities and refinancing conditions to investor requirements. However, there will obviously be no mutualisation of the credit risk connected with the changeover to the single currency. Issuance of euro-denominated bonds by the member states will probably affect the issuing policies of other major borrowers; the commitment of the issuing state could provoke the changeover of all markets to the euro. And even if issuing policies are independent from monetary policy, issuance of short-term debt instruments in euros is bound to facilitate management of the monetary policy for the single currency by the ESCB, which will be able to use such securities as collateral. Thus, the public administrations will begin to handle a significant transaction volume in euros from 1 January 1999 onwards.

By contrast, the conclusions of the Madrid summit do not explain how the existing public debt stock is to be treated. Hence, each member state will remain free to determine the conversion schedule of its own debt stock: market pressure (notably demand for liquidity) and issuing techniques (notably assimilation) could lead to rapid conversion of the existing debt stock. France was the first to announce that it would proceed to do so from 1 January 1999 onwards. Pressure from operators, whether financial or not, should prompt most states to do the same, even if this cumbersome operation has to be spread over several weeks or months. However, tradable public debt is unlikely to be distinguished according to whether it is paperless or not, or according to the bearer.

Public acceptability

Thanks to their close relation with the general public, the administrations hold the key to acceptability of the single currency. While acceptance of the euro by the citizens of certain countries will depend on the confidence inspired by the monetary and budgetary stability policy pursued by the member states participating in the third stage, harmonious transition of national currencies to the single currency will also depend on many practical aspects controlled by the administrations.

Conversion of the national currency to the euro and double price tags will not become an issue before the introduction of cash. However, it is linked to determination of conversion rates between various national currencies (at the latest by the start of 1999), rules for rounding off figures (which must be geared to prevent price hikes) and, lastly, supervision of double price tags. All these tasks are part of an administration's duties. Public utilities (water, gas, electricity, telecommunications, and so on), regardless of their management method (public or private), will probably have to start accustoming their clientele as early as 1999 to euro-denominated payments, by showing prices in this currency on invoices still denominated in national currency. Tax and social security administrations will probably have to do the same.

Acceptability of the euro naturally requires acceptability of the cash by which it will be represented. The considerable progress made by specialists must now result in information for the general public, which may be helped by the choice of design and graphics for notes and coins by the European Monetary Institute and by the mint administrations of the countries concerned.

Public administrations are also key players in the area of redistribution, whether by taxes or, especially, by social security. Problems connected with indirect taxes are closely linked to euro-denominated price tags. As regards direct taxes, the most delicate period will be the watershed year in which taxes are collected in the euro while fiscal statements were still drawn up in the national currency. Tax adjustments applied in the former national currencies after final introduction of the euro will also call for educational efforts. As with taxation of private citizens, social security will not be changed over before the new notes and coins are introduced. In fact, social benefits are often paid in cash to many households and involve many small transactions. Regardless of the social security management method of the member states, it is necessary to prepare the staff of these agencies and to define their new rules relatively soon.

In general, non-financial administrations still have only a vague idea of the scope of the change brought about by the introduction of the euro. In addition to the social administrations, educational departments will naturally facilitate the use of the euro by a population which, though outwardly less resistive to the single currency than the older population, can act as a driving force. Agencies attached to government, most of which are in direct contact with the public, will play a central role: ministerial departments or local authorities which contribute to the budget of such agencies could well link their subsidies to actions in favour of the euro.

All these actions must be underpinned by an overall communication plan. This plan, which should cover the entire period until the introduction of euro cash, should already be prepared, notably based on regular opinion polls. It must be targeted at all publics. Even if necessarily national, it must align with the communication of other member states. It needs to be open-ended. The role of central government, whose ministry-specific communication plans must fit into the overall communication plan, will consist of three parts: educating the general public in the overall process, and the way in which public administration will manage the changeover (as regards taxation, social security, dual-pricing, etc.), and finally briefing local government and other agencies in direct contact with the public.

Public administration has a demanding task ahead. But successful monetary reforms in the past (such as the decimalisation of the British and Irish pounds) show that the changeover can be completed without trauma if managed in a long-term perspective and in close collaboration between all economic and social operators. The six-year period from start to completion of the process seems a reasonable time to prepare for the changeover. Given that this challenge coincides with a complete review of the roles and working methods of most public administrations, it comes as both an opportunity and a major risk.

Chapter Twenty Three

Case Study: Consumers

Dick Westendorp

Economic and Monetary Union has considerable consequences for consumers. Although EMU will take effect from 1999, consumers will have to wait until 2002 before they can really pay in euro notes and coins. It will, however, be possible to do bank transfers before 2002.

This chapter deals with the expected advantages for the consumer, the expected bottle-necks and possible solutions for these problems. Finally some comments will be made on the role consumer organisations can play in the transition period.

No more currency conversion, exchange rate risks and exchange costs

People will no longer have to convert currency when travelling from one EMU state to another. There will no longer be exchange costs and exchange rates. The amount saved is considerable. This can be illustrated by the well known example in which a consumer travels from Amsterdam to the fourteen other capitals in the European Union. He does not purchase anything, he just changes his money into the local currency. After visiting these capitals he returns to Amsterdam with less than half the original amount.

Cross border payments are still expensive and take a long time compared to domestic payments. As a study conducted by Retail Banking Research for the European Commission in August 1994 shows, the total cost of carrying out credit transfers remains very high — at ecu 25.4 on average for transferring an amount equivalent to ecu 100. Other problems concerning cross border payments are the transparency (according to the same study, written information was completely lacking in 46% of bank branches surveyed and only 14% of branches provided full, written information), time for execution of the transfers and lack of an adequate redress systems. It is hoped that the proposed directive on cross border payments will improve the situation. The euro and EMU will most certainly help because of the emergence of a true single market in financial matters. This is likely to imply that cross-border transfers need no longer be treated differently from domestic transfers.

Lower prices through increased competition and transparency
Monetary union will be the completion of the internal market, providing industry with economies of scale in production and distribution. Moreover the direct costs of production will diminish. The European Commission has calculated that industry spends ecu 19 - 23 bn for accounting, price lists and exchanging money. These costs will diminish considerably once EMU has been established and consumers should also benefit from the advantages of the single currency. These savings should be reflected in the prices of goods and services. Using one currency will also increase cross-border transparency and make it easier to compare prices. This in turn will enhance competition and the increased competition may lead to lower prices and/or better quality.

But, in the short term, only the advantage of not having to deal with exchange rates will be visible to the consumer. The other advantages will only be noticeable in the longer term. And these benefits may not even be passed on to the consumer. In order for consumers to have confidence in European integration they must be able to see the benefits of integration. Without support from the European citizens the internal market and EMU will never meet their expectations.

On the negative side, however, consumers will lose their well-known and familiar terms of reference for assessing the price of goods and services and the comparative prices of competing products. In the beginning they will have the same experience as being abroad. They will have to calculate every price to assess if something is cheap or expensive. The whole notion of expensive or inexpensive will have to be acquired again. In cases where the value of the euro unit is larger than that of the national currency unit, consumers may have the impression that products and services have become cheaper, and vice versa. This is particularly a problem for the elderly and less-educated.

The transition to a single currency may well be used to cover hidden price rises. It is essential that the costs of transition are kept to a minimum. During the transition a single conversion rate should be used to convert a national currency into the euro. No extra costs should be charged. Once the euro becomes legal tender, prices will have to be transposed from the old currency into the new. Undoubtedly prices will have to be rounded. Consumers are suspicious that the prices will all be rounded up. They will also be concerned that the price of products and services will rise. This may be quite easy to do as the transition period will most probably be chaotic. Consumentenbond, the largest Dutch consumer organisation, conducted a euro survey among its members in March 1996. The fear of hidden price rises and misuse of the transition period was one of the main concerns of those interviewed.

A pressing question is what will happen with long-term contracts, like insurance, mortgages and pensions. Will these lose their value once the euro replaces the old currency? This would cause tremendous uncertainty amongst consumers. Moreover it would lead to chaos if all contracts had to be renegotiated. And most important, it would lead to uncertainty of the value of long-term contracts. In the above survey the concern about continuity of contracts was significant. However, the proposed Council regulations concerning the introduction of the euro are designed to eliminate such problems, and therefore fears.

The need for information
Acceptance of the euro by the public at large is an essential condition for its successful introduction. To achieve this, further analysis of consumer needs and requirements is imperative. Moreover, consumers have a right to know completely about the consequences of the changeover. There is a need for information on why the euro is necessary and what are the consequences for consumers. The information should be simple, understandable, free-of-charge, practical, useful, easily accessible and available to all. Every method of communication and technology should be used in order to reach every consumer, even if they are still not sufficiently aware of the decisions laid down in the Maastricht Treaty. Consumers will only prepare themselves when they know that the process is irrevocable. Clear information will enable consumers to accept the euro quicker and fewer problems will occur. The evidence is that when consumers

have the feeling that they are well-informed about EMU and the euro, they will have a more positive attitude towards them. This should be a stimulus for providing information to consumers in every stage of the transition. The information, however, should meet certain standards.

Information should be tailor-made, and geared towards specific groups. This is important in order to make sure that no group of consumers is overlooked. Some categories of consumers are likely to have greater problems getting used to the euro, like elderly people, handicapped, migrants and people with financial difficulties. Within this groups especially, the risk of a knowledge gap and Euro-scepticism is present. It is a shared responsibility for government and all parties involved in the transition to ensure that these groups are not neglected.

Use of new technologies
In order to ease the transition process it has been suggested that physical cash should be phased out. Electronic money, on the other hand, should be launched as the new payment method and maximum use should be made of new technologies to ease the transition. However, this must only be an option. The introduction of new means of payment is not neutral for the consumer. Additional costs and new conditions of use are often imposed on the consumer. Those who want to continue to use cash must not be prevented from doing so by the transition to a new currency. The are three main practical reasons why new technologies should only be optional:

- new technologies are not accessible to all consumers. Moreover these new techniques should be assessed for privacy, cost and user-friendliness;

- what about payments from consumer to consumer? For example how will a parent give his child pocket money?

- a total dependency on electronic payment systems, with no alternatives, should be avoided. In case of a power cut no payments whatsoever will be possible. And that is not in the interest of the consumer.

During the transition the official conversion rate should be used to convert a national currency to the euro. Using a different rate should be prohibited and so should imposing additional charges for the one-off conversion.

Various economic operators including banks and retailers will incur costs as a result of the transition. The situation in which these costs are seen as a justification for immediate price rises must be avoided at all times. With suitable planning, many of these costs can be treated as an investment in new technology. Some banks and companies will manage the transition better than others. It is important that their good efforts should have a positive effect on competition: this will not happen if there is an automatic or implicit assumption that transition costs imply price rises. The Commission's Directorate-General for Competition (DG IV) will need to be particularly vigilant to guard against any concerted arrangements to raise prices.

Consumers will suspect that the transition to the euro will be used to cover hidden price rises. There is a possibility that retailers will take the opportunity to raise prices. Whatever the outcome, the consumer should know. In order to inform consumers and officials whether the transition period is being taken advantage of, widespread price surveys before, during and after the transition should take place. The results should be published and firm action should be taken when necessary.

Consumers will need a considerable period of time to adjust their price reference values from the national currencies to the new one. Dual pricing will therefore be required for a while. Consideration should be given to starting with dual pricing before Phase C, so that consumers can get used to the euro. The objectives of dual pricing are twofold: to provide consumer information and to facilitate the acceptance of the euro by the man in the street. This will be important as people will suspect that the rounding of prices will hide unfair inflation.

The role of consumer organisations
The role of consumer organisations cannot be underestimated. Adequate support from the population is to the benefit of the governments as well. This, however, will not be easy. Consumers have little faith in the internal market and Europe. They have not seen much of the promised gains from the internal market as yet.

Consumer organisations will observe the transition closely. When suspicion arises of unlawful price-rises or when it becomes obvious that the consumer will have to pay unilaterally for the transition, consumer organisations will not hesitate to notify the competent authorities. In order to be successful, some sort of legislation which prohibits hidden and unjustified price increases, should be put in place. Research into how the process is getting along does not necessarily have to be done by consumer organisations, but the results should be made available to the public and the intermediaries. It should also be made possible to adjust along the way. This implies, however, that legislation or other actions should be able to take place quickly, without the lengthy discussions well known in the European Union. Consumer organisations will undoubtedly influence the decision-making process by means of campaigning activities and consultations. Consumer organisations consider it their task to give information and education before, during and after the transition period. Consumer organisations have ample experience in informing the consumer.

In summary, consumers may benefit from the euro. But to enable the consumer to benefit, the bottlenecks described above, need to be overcome. Clear information is essential. Information campaigns must be timely, continuous, comprehensive and flexible, based on a clear understanding of consumer concerns. In addition the economic interests of consumers should be taken into account. This should be done through double pricing, continuity of legal contracts as well as transparency and competing markets. The transition is a great challenge for all partners concerned. Many interests are at stake. Consumer interests as well. Consumer organisations consider themselves as an important player in the transition process for which the preparations are in full swing.

Chapter Twenty Four

Case Study: The Dutch Experience

Henk Brouwer

The Dutch government, through a special National Forum on the euro, is doing its utmost to be among the states that introduce the euro on 1 January 1999. There is broad popular support. According to recent opinion surveys, the Dutch population agrees with the economic and political goal of achieving Economic and Monetary Union along the lines agreed at the European Council in Madrid in December 1995. Below, the Dutch preparations for the changeover to the euro will be clarified. Some preparations concern policy measures, others are of a technical nature. The latter come increasingly to the fore, since time is limited before the third stage of EMU starts on 1 January 1999. Although the emphasis of this contribution is therefore on the technical preparations, one or two policy questions which sometimes cause confusion will also be addressed.

Macroeconomic policy
The idea that a stable macroeconomic environment is a precondition for sound economic performance is widely shared within the EU. The Maastricht criteria are essential in supporting the convergence of key economic factors towards healthy levels. In the Netherlands, a consistent monetary policy centred on maintaining a stable exchange rate vis-à-vis the German mark as well as stringent budgetary policies resulting in a budget deficit well below 3% GDP in 1997, determine a stable macro-economic environment. To those who wonder whether European budgetary policies are overly rigid because of the need to comply with the convergence criteria, our answer would be that the need for budgetary consolidation is inevitable, even without the emergence of EMU. Reducing fiscal deficits and debt levels is necessary in most of the member states in order to reduce the burden on monetary policy and to anticipate the budgetary effects of an ageing population.

Although fiscal consolidation reduces effective demand, it can also contribute to a better economic performance, since improving the soundness of public finance enhances the credibility of government policy, and therefore reduces interest rates. In so doing economic growth can be stimulated, probably even in the short run.[1] In recent history there are quite a few examples that support the idea that there is no contradiction in reducing public expenditure and stimulating economic growth. A point in case is the Dutch experience during the second half of the 1980s, when the budget deficit was reduced while maintaining a buoyant economic growth performance.

The fact that there are several underlying arguments in favour of improving public finance, does not mean, of course, that the movement towards EMU did not play a role in the consolidation process. Indeed, it was a welcome help and an essential precondition. Before joining the hard currency club it is clear that countries need to act according to the rules of the club in order not to hamper other members.

The effect on budgetary policies is only one example of how EMU influences policy. Another important effect is that EMU rules out competitive devaluations vis-à-vis EMU partners. Accordingly, competition is encouraged. EMU is therefore one of the underlying reasons why structural policies have become increasingly important in the Netherlands.

Technical preparations

Policy preparations will continue, but technical preparations have also started. The government considers these preparations as crucial, as apart from the need for technical preparations similar to those of large enterprises, the government is also responsible for a smooth introduction of the euro in society.

Most technical preparations need to be completed by 1 January 2002. Why has the Dutch government already entered into activities? There are two main reasons.

First, after the decision in early 1998 of which countries are allowed to participate in EMU, there will not be much time left. This is especially true for legislation, since it takes approximately a year and a half to pass legislation. It is essential to have worked out plans which can be implemented immediately after the formal decision on which countries participate. In this context, it is worthwhile considering a lesson from the ancient Romans: *si vis pacem, para bellum*. Or, in other words, a country has to be well prepared to avoid disturbing events before entering into new demanding tasks, such as the introduction of the euro.

Second, listing activities early is also necessary, because some activities need to be completed as early as 1999. Without a proper survey one might forget one or two of those activities. Generally speaking, activities which need to be completed by 1999 should be started without delay. For example, the Banking Act, which determines the position of the Dutch central bank, needs revision well before the start of the third phase of EMU.

Ministry of Finance

Preparations are coordinated by the Ministry of Finance. Within the ministry there is a departmental task force developing a scenario for the introduction of the euro. 'Account-managers' in different parts of the ministry are involved in order to list activities, identify possible problems etc. Listing indicates that most activities have not yet been started. This does not mean that the preparations have no practical consequences so far. As mentioned before, some activities already need to be started. Even more important, however, is the fact that the introduction of the euro can be anticipated by means of the so-called euro test. The euro test implies that large scale investment projects in the field of automation are valued along the following lines. Either it must be demonstrated that the introduction of the euro does not influence the project under review at all, or the project must take account, as much as possible, of the introduction of the new currency. The underlying idea is that it is usually much more convenient, and therefore cheaper to anticipate future demands before the project is set up than to adapt the system afterwards.

The departmental task-force is developing a scenario in which all euro related activities of the Ministry of Finance are embodied. The scenario clearly links related activities and identifies interdependencies. One interesting example regards coins. Coin production cannot be started before the technical characteristics of the euro coins are known. These characteristics depend on the design, which will be decided after a European design competition ending in early 1997. After this decision, preparations for production can start. The actual production of all coins takes place between early 1998 and

1 January 2002, when euro coins are to be introduced. In the Netherlands no less than 1.5 bn coins have to be produced in three years time; a real challenge for the producers of these coins.

Coordination within different parts of government

Not only within the Ministry of Finance, but in all Dutch ministries, task forces have been established to survey the technical consequences of the introduction of the euro as regards their own operations. The activities of these task forces are coordinated in the so-called Interdepartmental Working-group Euro. Working together, members became increasingly aware of the fact that ministries are confronted with similar problems. These problems fall into three different categories: public relations, accounting and legal issues.

Since ministries are already cooperating in the field of public relations, questions as to how to communicate the scenario of the introduction of the euro to the general public are dealt with in the existing framework. For both the other categories working groups have been set up.

The working group on accounting issues is preparing the changeover of computerised accounting systems to the euro. This is an enormous operation, since there are many different computer systems, often linked together. The working hypothesis for all these automation related issues is that all different parts of the Dutch government, including social security, will change to the euro on 1 January 2002.

The working group on legal issues focuses on modifications of existing legislation. Without adaptation confusion might arise. For example, a rounded guilder figure in a particular Act should be converted into a rounded euro figure. The mere use of fixed conversion rates is too simple a solution. Of course, there are also some specific Acts which have to undergo major changes. One example is the Banking Act mentioned earlier.

The results of the working groups on legal and accounting issues, the activities in the field of public relations and major results from the departmental task forces will all be put together in an interdepartmental scenario to be presented to the Dutch Council of Ministers. As a result the Dutch government will be well informed about the preparations of the administration for the introduction of the euro. This scenario is a guide, and will of course be adapted as new information becomes available.

National Forum

As pointed out before, the government has a responsibility for the smooth introduction of the new currency. Therefore, the Dutch government deems it important to encourage public support for this major event and to support preparations for the introduction of the euro in varying sectors of society. With a view to these goals, the Dutch government established the National Forum for the Introduction of the Euro last February, only three months after the European Council in Madrid. The Forum's operational aims are threefold:

- to support a two way exchange of information;
- to signal possible solutions for commonly felt problems;
- to coordinate publicity efforts.

All major institutions need to be well informed for a successful introduction of the euro. The fact that the members of the National Forum hold pivotal positions in Dutch society implies that they can spread information easily to the organisations they represent. At the same time the members of the National Forum are well placed to communicate problems or other signals from their sector or institution both to the government to other members.

The exchange of information is closely related to the second aspect: finding solutions for commonly felt problems. Practical problems need practical, not ivory tower solutions. If one institution has developed a useful approach for certain technical problems, other participants may profit from the benefits of that solution as well. If there are several options, the government should be well informed about the consequences of each of them.

The third aim deals directly with public relations. In the Netherlands, popular support for EMU does not seem to be a major problem; according to a recent opinion survey from the Dutch central bank, 70% of the Dutch regard the euro to be at least as acceptable as the guilder. Nevertheless, information to the general public plays an important role. The National Forum has decided to set up a working party on this issue, in which public relations officers in all participating sectors and institutions take part. The working party coordinates publicity activities. The guiding principle is that each organisation remains responsible for its own PR. Nevertheless, it is generally recognised that companies and citizens should obtain a correct and consistent picture of all the relevant issues.

The National Forum is scheduled to meet four times a year. Every meeting consists of a 'tour de table' for information exchange and a discussion about a major topic: PR, legal issues, and the financial markets context.

The National Forum agreed that it is too early to approach the general public with a mass-media campaign on EMU. As many practical implications are still being considered, a mass-media campaign would lack substance and would be labelled by some as propaganda. The general public will be approached modestly until the final decision is made in early 1998. Having said that, it would be wrong, and probably dangerous not to inform the general public at all. It was considered to be extremely important to inform both the public and businesses as soon as possible about the actual plans and their consequences. This was deemed necessary both to give correct, factual information and to take away unnecessary fears and misunderstandings.

The discussion of legal issues feeds directly into this need for better information. It deals with questions as to what will happen to contracts in national currency, what will happen to contracts in ecus and to mortgages, and many other questions. The National Forum will answer these questions systematically and the outcome of this discussion will be used to inform society.

The National Forum has been a success so far. Although some of the participants have some reservations about certain aspects of EMU, all feel that we should take care of the process in a smooth, efficient manner. The ancient Roman forum was the place where one could influence political, social and commercial life. The National Forum may not formally be in charge of anything, but it is the place where major stakeholders can understand and often influence the political, social and commercial implications of the introduction of the euro.

In the Netherlands during the beginning of the 1990s the macroeconomic policy improvements have been supported by the determination to strengthen the economy in order to comply with the convergence criteria laid down in the Maastricht Treaty. Since the actual starting day of EMU is approaching, the technical preparations increasingly require attention. Without organising the adaptation of, among other activities, legislation and accounting systems, a country is unable to introduce the euro, regardless of the soundness of its macroeconomic policies. A practical approach, using scenarios, seems to be fruitful, as the case of the Netherlands illustrates. A platform with high level representatives of all parts of society, such as the Dutch National Forum, can also be a very valuable instrument in preparing a country for the major changes in economic life resulting from the introduction of the euro.

---

[1] Francesco Giavazzi and Marco Pagano, *Non-Keynesian Effects of Fiscal Policy Changes: International Evidence and the Swedish Experience*, 1995, National Bureau for Economic Research (NBER) Working Paper no. 5332.

Chapter Twenty Five

Case Study: Preparing Public Administration

Rolf Kaiser

As of 15 November 1996, twelve out of the fifteen member states of the European Union have set up formal task forces or units to coordinate the adaptation of their public administrations to the euro. Universally, this effort has been entrusted to the finance ministries as the focal point for discussions and decisions within the public sector and between the public and private sectors.

In a number of countries, these activities started immediately after the publication of the European Commission's Green Paper in mid-1995, with the rest following suit after the decisions of the Madrid European Council in December. Characteristically, the structure of work in member states involves four main areas:

Organisation. As all parts of administration, including regional and local, will be affected by the changeover to the euro, national euro-coordinators at finance ministry level frequently sought a Cabinet decision or a directive issued by the head of government, in order to be able to extract the necessary information from all agencies concerned. As the necessary actions to be undertaken government-wide will be counted by the thousands, several countries have introduced or are examining the use of PC-based tracking systems.

Legislative work. Most governments are currently in the process of running an exhaustive analysis of all existing legislation in order to identify all texts containing monetary data. The approach used is two-fold:

- all legal texts containing national currency denominations without a concrete amount will usually be changed into the euro denomination with a single, catch-all law;

- such legal texts that contain an amount (for example, tax allowances, tax thresholds, fines, fees and charges) are often being treated separately, as a decision will have to be taken whether to convert national currencies simply into euros according to the conversion rate established by unanimous decision of the Ecofin of the 'in' states on the first day of monetary union, 1 January 1999, or whether to decide about a new euro amount politically.

Information technology. With many public administrations now working with several generations of hardware and software, the task is complex; governments have realised that timely preparation is necessary to avoid last-minute bottlenecks. As the transitional period will require some double-denomination operations, one of the main development thrusts is the modification or the preparation of public sector software capable of converting and displaying the euro as well as the national denomination from 1 January 1999.

Information and communications. While very few governments have so far undertaken information campaigns for the broad public, almost all member states have entered into a close dialogue with the financial and business communities as well as with associations representing the interests of consumers. The typical mid-term goal of many governments is to eventually issue practical manuals before the start of monetary union, explaining all aspects of the changeover, be they mandated by EU legislation or by supplementary national legislation. Several member states have agreed on joint communications activities with the Commission, and others are preparing similar plans.

The European Commission's services are furthermore in close contact with national public administration coordinators, a mutual exchange of experience and ideas is taking place continuously. Two meetings addressing the above topics have so far taken place in Brussels in 1996, with more to follow.

Chapter Twenty Six

Case Study: Trade Associations

David Croughan

Trade associations will play a key role as one of the multipliers in disseminating awareness of the changeover to the single currency, providing information, raising key questions and providing answers to the vast array of companies which must make the necessary changes to all their systems and procedures by 2002 at the latest. One of our primary concerns as a business representative body is to ensure that all companies start to address the implications for their business early rather than wait until 1999, or worse still, 2002. For some companies it will make good sense to move early to use the euro, either because of substantial treasury gains or because their links in the business chain to major customers or suppliers would make sound economic sense. For others it would make more sense to delay. But each company should come to its decision as a result of investigation, not by default.

To date very few companies have actually begun the process of formulating a changeover plan. In part that is to be expected because the credibility that EMU is happening is only now beginning to gather pace. The Irish Business and Employers Confederation (IBEC) undertook a survey in Ireland in autumn 1996 showed that although 89% of firms surveyed believed EMU would happen and 91% were in favour of Ireland joining, 65% did not believe it would happen on time (defined as within the first six months of 1999). So even now we still have to get across to business the reality of the EMU timetable. This must emanate largely from statements of governments, central banks and the Commission. If these sources of 'inside' information cast any doubts on EMU, they are often interpreted by the business community as suggesting the timetable for EMU is off. The IGC in Dublin in December ought to provide a further push of credibility.

The IBEC survey also gives some indication of the size of the task ahead. Only 7% of companies had appointed someone to manage the changeover to the single currency; not surprisingly only 4% had any strategy for the changeover or had made any assessment of the financial impact of the changeover. Lastly, when asked whether they thought their company would change over their systems early to the euro, of the 30% of managers who expressed an opinion, two thirds thought they would changeover in the first year. If the Irish situation is typical of Europe, then a lot of companies have only two years in which to prepare.

Communicating

There are a number of levels of communication that trade associations must become involved in if companies are to make the changeover in the most efficient manner possible.

The first task is to spread as far and wide the reality of EMU, the credibility of the starting date, the context within which EMU is happening, the three stages of EMU from the naming of the countries to the locking of exchange rates to the introduction of the single currency and the withdrawal of national currencies. It is important to explore what kind of transactions are likely to take place in euros in the early stages and how much business could be involved in euro transactions in the period 1999-2002. There is a need to explain that it will be possible to carry out inter-company transactions in euros well before the physical notes and coins are available. This leads to a general awareness of what this might mean for pricing policies and for legal contracts which either currently exist or will be taken out from now on and span the next few years. Companies need to think of their position in the market and assess the financial, accounting and software impact of the transfer to euros.

In bringing these general areas to the attention of companies, two important messages need to be got across. First, the urgency to establish a team with backing from the top to make initial assessments of the company's choice about whether to change early or to wait. The second is to ensure that companies have some idea of their own in-house capabilities to make the changes or whether such services need to be bought in. Of special importance is the need to ensure that companies inclined to wait realise there could be a spike in the demand for software or legal expertise which could jeopardise their timetable or possibly prove costly.

There is recent experience for managing this kind of mass information campaign. In the late 1980s, trade federations had the task of communicating the implications of the single market to firms. This involved preparing a series of specialised information packs regarding the general overview, taxation, transport, standards, finance and taxation. We held numerous seminars, giving slide presentations and we limited the seminars to useful working numbers of not more than fifty. In some cases we worked with local Chambers of Commerce, sometimes with clients of banks or accounting firms as well as directly through our own membership. In some states larger conferences may be more appropriate. In all the seminars we always devoted one to 'what business must do' and this was always the one that evoked the most interest and helped companies develop a starting point and a checklist of the implications.

The general communication exercise on EMU, likewise, should involve a large number of seminars, as well as business-oriented booklets on the implications and checklists of what companies need to do. We have a good example of such a booklet published by the Association for the Monetary Union of Europe. A major element of the seminars must be that they are two-way: part of the exercise is to obtain feedback of opinions and problems. This helps the process of building up a national conversion plan. In the initial seminars our aim would be to give every company the framework of how to establish a changeover plan at company level. On the feedback side, we will be looking for indications of the corporate timetable, what business requires of government, its opinions on dual pricing and any problems foreseen.

The onus is very much on trade associations to be the go-between with business and government. This requires passing on to officials in public administration reactions to government policy and to articulate the requirements of business in making the changeover as cost effectively as possible and in harness with the national changeover timetable. All member states have been urged to establish a national platform for the changeover; it is incumbent on trade associations to make sure they are prominent on such platforms and that they bring business needs to the attention of government. In Ireland the Department of Finance has set up an embryo national platform on which IBEC has a seat and we have also established contact with the corporate planning department of the Revenue Commissioners. Trade associations ought to try to establish the real demands of industry rather than all encompassing wish-lists. For example, the Revenue Commissioners have expressed a willingness to meet, as far as possible, the requirements of those companies which would want to file returns before 2002. It is quite unlikely that they could deal with every company in euros in 1999 but they are willing to try to meet the needs of those companies who would really gain from moving to the euro in 1999. Part of our input would be to try to establish realistically how many companies that will be.

There will also need to be liaison between government and the retail sector as to what demands will be made on companies to display dual pricing and the possible implications for cash registers, and so forth. There is a happy balance between ensuring customer confidence and onerous and possibly confusing dual pricing requirements. As the process develops, federations will play a vital role in being the instrument of dissemination and feedback.

Trade federations must also work closely with the European Commission in obtaining and understanding the most up-to-date information so that it can be disseminated to industry. The Commission must play its part here in providing as much information as possible with regular updatings. As with national governments, federations should feed back to the Commission industry concerns or suggestions. It may well become important that the Commission ensures that member states are moving to the single currency at roughly the same speed in order to avoid inefficiencies. Trade associations should alert the Commission of cross-border inefficiencies that may be encountered.

Trade federations will have a strong role to play in inter-business communications. The most obvious example is forging a link between what business will expect from the banking system compared with what facilities the banking system is prepared to offer. For example, some companies may wish the banking system to do all their conversions between the national currency and the euro; the banks may not be able or willing to undertake such tasks, or may make significant charges. Trade federations must be prepared to work with banks to facilitate the essential link with business.

There is also a need to build links between software companies and business. To date, software companies seem to have developed few plans about how they will undertake the very substantial demands on their services. On the other hand, some companies appear almost complacent that software companies will deliver an off-the-shelf solution to all their problems. Federations must encourage business to discover and make known their requirements to software companies and keep pace with developments in this important area.

The accounting profession, too, has a major role to play. Small companies in particular may not be able to afford consultants but they all must have auditors. Federations can work with audit companies in bringing the message to business.

Federations can act as a link or bridge between businesses providing services germane to the changeover and the rest of the business sector. As part of this process we are exploring the possibility of working with a handful of companies from different sectors and making the changeover with the help of professionals. This might prove a very useful exercise in producing a model changeover plan that small companies could adopt. It is our intention to work with the banks, accountants, software and legal companies to develop our checklists for action and to hold joint seminars. Federations should also act as the bridge between business and consumer groups where information needs may clash with practical or cost considerations.

As companies set up their own single currency conversion team, federations ought to be able to act as an initial facilitator to ensure that all the various elements are taken on board. It would be particularly useful if federations facilitated a number of pilot changeover strategies by way of management briefings, or teasing out the correct timing of the changeover for the least cost while bearing in mind the commercial needs. Some federations undertake a variety of training activities as part of their overall services. EMU must become part of this activity.

Studies

Federations should be undertaking studies of various aspects of EMU and how it will impact on different businesses. In Ireland the government commissioned the Economic and Social Research Institute to undertake a study of the implications of EMU on the Irish economy. Our federation is making use of this study, especially where we see possible vulnerable businesses or sectors. Our own federation has also published a study of the impact of EMU on business. Clearly there will be different issues in different countries. In Ireland for example there is great concern that sterling may not be party to EMU and could devalue. As the UK is a major customer for certain sectors, we are looking at how these sectors may be able to respond flexibly to a possible sterling devaluation. We are currently considering what the impact of EMU may be on the island economy of Ireland, both North and South, under the scenario of the UK and Ireland being party to EMU and, alternatively, with the UK outside.

Federations should keep up-to-date with business opinion through surveys and interviews. This has a dual purpose: questionnaires prompt companies to think of issues they may not have thought of; and they provide useful up-to-date information on business needs.

Communication methods
The following is a brief outline of the methods of communication that we in IBEC intend to follow.

- An information booklet outlining the EU changeover scenario, the government's national intentions and the implications for business. Essentially this booklet provides necessary information and a checklist of what companies must do.

- Prepare series of information slides and hold numerous seminars. For Ireland, we believe there should be a relatively small number of companies at each seminar. Distribute videos or CD ROMs which we hope the Commission will provide.

- Institute a quarterly EMU bulletin so that companies will be provided with up-to-date information on developments as they occur, so that these can be taken on board at company level.

- Maintain an up-to-date information source on the Internet.

- Set up a hotline to answer queries by the Confederation's team of specialists by both telephone and electronic mail.

- Provide briefing and training sessions at company level.

- Conduct ongoing surveys to keep up to date with developments and also continue to keep the issues in front of companies.

Chapter Twenty Seven

Conclusions

Graham Bishop, José Pérez, Sammy van Tuyll

This book is addressed especially to those who have to prepare their companies for the changeover to the euro. The experience of those who have already started down the road may provide food for thought. It should also prompt policymakers, as well as a wider public.

Given the magnitude of the changeover, and its unprecedented nature, communication among all stakeholders in society will be essential. The managers of companies have a particularly clear obligation to their shareholders but the obligations in the public sector are not so clear cut. The annual report to shareholders seems a natural vehicle for a formal review of the issues facing each company.

The contributions from our expert authors have shown that there are a number of policy issues which need to be tackled and we list some of those that are particularly striking:

Consumers

- everyone agrees that dual labelling is essential, but there are strong differences of opinion about whether it should be made obligatory — and, if so, how. Can competition in the market place ensure that adequate information is provided? Or will legislation be needed? If so, could it balance rigour with sufficient flexibility?

- 'dual legal tender' may pose enormous practical problems to handlers of cash — stores, banks, vending machine operators. One solution is to shorten the period of dual legal tender to the point where it is a 'legal big bang'. This would leave businesses free to accept payment in both currencies but only pay out the new euro money. Otherwise, huge queues at supermarket check-outs may not enhance the public acceptance of the euro;

Enterprises

- changing over on 1 January may suit accountants' year-end balance sheets but could pose a severe challenge to a smooth changeover at retail level because it is the peak retailing season. The February (or October) low points would be better;

- vending machine operators face particular problems and may need special treatment to avoid disrupting the public. Specifically, the note and coin technical specifcations need to be agreed and published as soon as possible.

- is there enough software and computer programming capacity available in Europe to deal with both EMU and the 'year 2000' problem?

Public administration

- The general public is likely to become much more aware of the imminence of the event if regular progress reports are published, and summarised in the media;

- taxation will be a key element and there is rising concern that EMU may crystallise a tax charge on unrealised gains. The temptation to accept a windfall improvement in public finances should be tempered by recognition of the potential ill-will that could be generated.

Financial Markets

- Conversion is now less than 500 business days away and the ISO code and symbol for the euro are not yet settled. However, the Commission proposal to use EUR as the code looks likely to be accepted and a quick decision on the symbol is also likely;

- the capital markets operate on a pan-European level and need a mechanism to ensure that all the national work on market conventions is circulated to all those with an interest.

This list of items for action is not exhaustive today and the list will get longer once the corporate sector begins serious analysis and planning. A trawl through annual reports for 1996 should be illluminating reading if the recommendations below are followed.

THE 1996 ANNUAL REPORT TO SHAREHOLDERS

Financial market participants, particularly in the bond markets, have recognised the probability that EMU will start on time in 1999. Because of the short time left for preparation, institutional shareholders may well start asking questions about a company's EMU strategy during 1997 as part of their evaluation of their company's management. The first source of information should be the annual report that will be published during 1997 relating to 1996. Shareholders will be looking for information at two levels:

- the mechanics of the actual changeover;

- the implications for the firm's business strategy.

Mechanics of the changeover
Shareholders are likely to want to know many of the following items:

- Has a project team been set up? Is it led at a high enough level? What areas are covered? These issues are discussed extensively in several chapters and in the case studies.

- What is the timetable for reporting?

(i) A conceptual assessment of the problems facing that particular firm? This should include the outline of the cost/benefit analysis.

(ii) When will the detailed plan for implementing the changeover be ready? The detail should include sufficient cost/benefit analysis to enable the firm to chose its optimum transition path: change over immediately; change at the last moment; or operate mainly in the old national currency but convert specific operations earlier. This plan should include a complete inventory of each action needed, by whom and when. It will undoubtedly require close consultation with the firm's lawyers and accountants as well as IT suppliers.

(iii) When will implementation begin, and when will it be completed? Is there any flexibility in the plan in case customers or suppliers change over at a faster pace? Can the suppliers of new equipment actually provide it within this schedule?

The next question is key: how much will it cost and how will this be financed? However, in this context, 'cost' is not a precise measure because there is an implication of wasted resources whereas, in reality, the firm's business strategy may be able to utilise much of the expenditure as normal capital investment.

It is certain that costs can be reduced by starting to plan the changeover early. Anticipation will save money. We would recommend to companies the 'euro-test' described on page 164.

Furthermore, the 'cost' to a retailer of new tills may be little more than computer programming changes because the normal replacement cycle of tills would lead to a complete renewal by 2002 anyway. For banks, the printing of new stationery is usually labelled as a 'cost of EMU' but can careful re-ordering reduce the actual wastage to modest amounts?

As each firm works through its own changeover plan, it may become apparent that industry-wide cooperation would smooth the way. Perhaps administrative action by national authorities is needed. Is the annual report a suitable vehicle to highlight such needs, perhaps as part of a campaign for necessary changes, but by whom, and by when, should the changes be made?

The firm's business strategy
Discussions about EMU and corporations are usually conducted in terms of the problems of the physical changeover. However, shareholders are likely to want reassurance about more fundamental implications for a firm's long term future:

- Can the firm gain a competitive edge by using the planning for the changeover to (i) redesign the marketing programme to take advantage of the single currency, in combination with the single market, to expand the home market free of the fear of foreign exchange costs and fluctuations; (ii) introduce a new cost reduction strategy. Some of these are widely discussed such as reducing the costs of treasury and accounting departments. How quickly can these cost savings be achieved?

It may be possible to reduce the number of bank relationships and achieve finer terms by concentrating business. Even smaller companies may be able to look for competing raw material suppliers in other participating countries without the risk of currency fluctuations, and difficulties in making the actual payments. Bringing forward the eventual investment in new equipment such as cash tills may produce straightforward efficiency gains as well as improving competitiveness. Can production be redesigned to meet psychological pricing points more quickly than the competition?

- Is any portion of a firm's business likely to lose out because of EMU? For example, does it profit from a cross-border pricing anomaly which will be difficult to sustain in a world of transparent prices? What is the strategy to reorientate the business to minimise any such effect?

- Is the firm's survival threatened if it cannot, or does not, change over in time? In a fiercely competitive market such as banking services, customers may simply switch their business away from a bank which cannot transact in euro. The damage could be substantial and permanent.

Shareholders will undoubtedly begin to wonder how a firm will benefit from all the aspects of EMU. So will employees, customers and suppliers because everyone will be looking at their own particular role in the chain of supply. A good strategy to deal with the mechanics of the conversion to the euro should be a launching pad for a broader strategic review to gain full advantage from a home market of 370 million customers. The annual report may be a particularly useful method of communicating to all those who are interested in the firm's long term welfare.

Chronology of EMU

TIMING	ACTIONS TO BE TAKEN	RESPONSIBILITY
December 1995	Adoption of the changeover scenario, including announcement of the deadline for the completion of the changeover (1 July 2002) and the name for the new currency	European Council
December 1996	Specification of the regulatory, organisation and logistical framework for the ECB/ESCB to perform its tasks in Stage Three	EMI
	Preparation of legislation related to the ECB/ESCB and to the introduction of the single currency	European Commission, EMI
Before the decision on participating member states	Conformity of national legislation [1]	Member states
START OF PHASE A As soon as possible in 1998	Decision on participating member states	European Council [2]
As soon as possible after the decision on participating member states	Appointment of Executive Board of the ECB	Member states [3]
	Set the day for the introduction of euro bank notes and coins.	ECB Council
	Start production of euro bank notes and coins	ESCB Council and member states
Up to 1 January 1999	Final preparation of the ECB/ESCB (i) Adoption of secondary legislation, including: key for capital subscription; collection of statistical information; minimum reserves of ECB; fines and penalties on undertakings;	European Council
	(ii) Rendering the ECB/ESCB operational: setting up the ECB; adoption of regulatory framework; testing monetary policy framework, etc	ECB/ESCB
START OF STAGE THREE AND PHASE B 1 January 1999	Irrevocable fixing of conversion rates and entry into force of legislation related to the introduction of the euro (legal status, continuity of contracts, rounding, etc)	European Council [4]

From 1 January 1999	(i) Definition and execution of the single monetary policy in euros	ESCB
	(ii) Conduct of foreign exchange operations in euros.	ESCB
	(iii) Operation of TARGET payment system.	ESCB
	(iv) Issue new public debt in euros	Member states
1 January 1999 to 1 January 2002 at the latest	(i) Exchange at par value of currencies with irrevocably fed conversion rates	ESCB
	(ii) Monitor changeover developments in the banking and finance industry	ESCB and EU and member state public authorities
	(iii) Assist the whole of the economy in an orderly changeover	ESCB and EU and member state public authorities
START OF PHASE C 1 January 2002 at the latest	(i) Start circulation of the euro bank notes and withdrawal of national bank notes	ESCB
	(ii) Start circulation of the euro coins and withdrawal of national coins	Member states [5]
END OF PHASE C 1 July 2002 at the latest [6]	(i) Complete changeover in the public administration	European Council; member states
	(ii) Cancel the legal tender status of national bank notes and coins	ESCB

[1] The Commission and EMI reports under Article 109j(l) shall include an examination of the compatibility between each member state's national legislation, including the statutes of each national central bank; and Articles 107 and 108 of the Treaty and the Statute of the ESCB (Article 108 provides that national legislation must be compatible with the Treaty and the Statute of the ESCB at the latest at the date of the establishment of the ESCB).

[2] In the composition of heads of state or government (Article 109j(4)).

[3] Governments of participating member states at the level of heads of state or government by common accord (Article 109l(1)).

[4] The Council shall act with the unanimity of the participating member states.

[5] Participating member states.

[6] Individual member states have the discretion to advance this date.

APPENDIX TWO

Necessary conditions for the adoption of the single currency

The necessary conditions for the adoption of a single currency, as laid down in the Treaty on European Union, are the following:[1]

A. Compatibility of the member state's national legislation, including the statutes of its national central bank, with Articles 107 and 108 of the Treaty and the Statute of the ECB. This essentially relates to the independence of the member state's Central Bank.

B. A high degree of sustainable convergence by reference to the fulfilment of the following four criteria:

1. The achievement of a high degree of price stability: an average rate of inflation that does not exceed by more than 1.5% that of, at most, the three best performing member states in terms of price stability.

2. The sustainability of the government's financial position; the government's budgetary position should not have an excessive deficit, for which there are two criteria:

   (i) the ratio of the planned or actual government deficit should not exceed 3% of GDP, unless either the ratio has declined substantially and continuously and reaches a level that comes close to this value, or, alternatively, the excess over the reference value is only exceptional and temporary and the ratio remains close to the reference value;

   (ii) the ratio of government debt to GDP should not exceed 60%, unless the ratio is sufficiently diminishing and approaching this value at a satisfactory pace.

3. The observance of the normal fluctuation margin provided for by the exchange-rate mechanism of the European Monetary System, for at least two years, without devaluing against the currency of any other member state.

4. The durability of convergence achieved by the member state and of its participation in the exchange-rate mechanism of the EMS, being reflected in the long-term interest-rate levels. These should not exceed by more than 2% that of, at most, the three best performing Member States in terms of price stability.

---

[1] This appendix takes several Treaty provisions together and paraphrases them. See the Treaty for the exact wording.